Diva

COOKING

VICTORIA BLASHFORD-SNELL & JENNIFER JOYCE

COOKING

UNASHAMEDLY GLAMOROUS PARTY FOOD

MITCHELL BEAZLEY

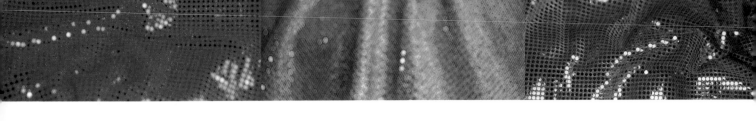

DEDICATION
To our boys – Julian, Jack, Patrick, Liam, and Riley

DIVA COOKING by Victoria Blashford-Snell & Jennifer Joyce
Photography by Georgia Glynn Smith

First published in Great Britain in 2001 by Mitchell Beazley, an imprint of
Octopus Publishing Group Ltd, 2-4 Heron Quays, London E14 4JP

This paperback edition first published in 2004

ISBN 1 84533 001 3

A CIP catalogue record for this book is available from the British Library. The author and publisher will be
grateful for any information that will assist them in keeping future editions up to date. Although all reasonable
care has been taken in the preparation of this book, neither the publisher nor the author can accept liability for
any consequences arising from the use thereof, or from the information contained therein.

Commissioning Editor: Rebecca Spry   Executive Art Editor: Phil Ormerod   Managing Editor: Jamie Grafton
Editors: Susan Fleming and Maggie Pannell   Design: The Senate   Proofreading: Jo Richardson
Production: Alex Wiltshire   Index: John Noble

Typeset in Eurostile

Printed and bound by Toppan Printing Company in China.

diva**contents**

these symbols are used in the recipe section:

 cooking tip

 double the quantity

 ingredients tip

 preparation tip

 serving tip

introduction 6

diva**canapés** 8

diva**tarts** 38

diva**meats** 54

diva**birds** 68

diva**fish** 82

diva**veggies** 98

diva**salads** 112

diva**extras** 128

diva**puddings** 140

diva**breads** 158

diva**cooking** 164

diva**parties** 168

index 176

diva**introduction**

We met over the cake counter. It was eight years ago at the infamous Books for Cooks on London's Portobello Road. Both of us were working in the tiny kitchen where recipes from hundreds of books are tested on eager customers. Our friendship first revolved around our mutual love of food, but later evolved to encompass the rest of our lives – our children, our husbands, our other interests. Yet all these years later, there is still one thing we focus on most: expanding our culinary skills through the constant, greedy quest for new ingredients, helpful techniques and useful insights. But we are frequently frustrated by the lack of detail in cookbooks and recipes. That's why we decided to write a different kind of book, a book that goes one step further.

In *Diva Cooking* we wanted not only to design delicious dishes, but also to teach you the secrets of preparing ahead, which recipes work well together and how best to handle presentation. That's why all the recipes feature 'Diva Dos' and 'Diva Don'ts', divulging essential information about how far in advance food can be made, potential pitfalls, doubling quantities and which colours or fresh herbs to use for garnishing.

Creating great dishes is to a large extent about choosing the right ingredients and understanding how to get the basics right, so we've also included ingredients spreads which advise on how to find the highest quality ingredients and how to cook with them. There are lots of powerful flavours in *Diva Cooking* too – whether it's sea salt used to enhance tastes or a new chilli paste, big tastes always go down well at a party. But knowing how to pair unusual flavours, spices and herbs isn't always obvious, so *Diva Cooking* features extra ingredients spreads on flavours as well as herbs and spices, to guide you on what they are and how to best use them.

Diva food is party food, and all the recipes in *Diva Cooking* have been created for parties of eight or more. They can all be eaten with a fork while standing and chatting, but most can also be enjoyed at sit-down dinner parties too. But figuring out a party menu that's balanced in terms of time and difficulty can be tricky. You'll find both simple and complex dishes in this book, and each recipe has estimated preparation and cooking times. That way you can choose a main dish that takes one hour with a salad that takes five minutes! No one should be chained to their kitchen for two days preparing for a party.

Diva Cooking doesn't do anything in a small way – we like bold flavours and sizzling style. We love recipes that make a statement, whether through using unusual ingredients, presenting classics beautifully or showcasing big, gutsy tastes. We believe food has to both look great and offer impressive flavour. Too often recipes concentrate on one characteristic at the expense of the other. In this book, every recipe guarantees both. And that's exactly what *Diva Cooking* is all about. Cook, eat and have fun. We do.

diva**canapés**

avocado-goat's cheese crostini with roasted cherry tomatoes

● Makes 20 canapés to serve 10　● Preparation: 20 minutes　● Cooking: 40 minutes

This unusual combination of avocado and mild goat's cheese works brilliantly as a crostini topping or dip. It looks beautiful and tastes delicious.

crostini

20 slices of day-old thin baguette, 1 cm (½ in) thick

olive oil

roasted cherry tomatoes

10 cherry tomatoes

olive oil

1 tbsp balsamic vinegar

salt and pepper

avocado puree

1 large ripe hass avocado

150 g (5½ oz) fresh, creamy goat's cheese

grated zest and juice of ½ lemon

1 tbsp olive oil

1 garlic clove, peeled

2 shakes of Tabasco sauce

salt and pepper

1 Preheat the oven to 180°C/ 350°F/Gas 4. To make the crostini, place the bread slices on a flat baking tray brushed with olive oil. Brush the bread with olive oil. Bake until crispy and golden brown, about 10 minutes. Set aside in a dry place until needed.

2 To roast the cherry tomatoes, preheat the oven to 150°C/ 300°F/Gas 2. Cut the tomatoes in half and place on a baking tray.

Drizzle with olive oil and balsamic vinegar, sprinkle with salt and pepper and roast for 30 minutes.

3 To make the avocado puree, place all the ingredients in a food processor and puree until smooth. Taste to check seasoning.

4 To assemble, place a tsp of the avocado puree on top of each crostini, and garnish with a roasted cherry tomato half.

diva**dos**

 Buy the avocados ahead of time to ensure they are ripe. Hass avocados are tastier and creamier, but other avocados can be used. Sun-blush tomatoes can be used instead of roasted cherry tomatoes. Choose the thinnest baguette available.

 You can make the crostini a week ahead and store in an airtight container. The avocado puree can be made 1 day ahead. Cover with clingfilm touching the puree to remove all air, then chill.

 Flat-leaf parsley or chopped chives can be used as an extra garnish.

diva**don'ts**

 Don't top the crostini more than 1 hour in advance. Don't leave the made crostini in direct sunlight.

golden shallot pancake with garlic and green olive tapenade

● Makes 25 pancakes to serve 10 -12   ● Preparation: 30 minutes   ● Cooking: 20 minutes

The sweet, velvety shallots provide a great base for the sharp, gusty tapenade.

shallot pancakes

15 g (½ oz) butter

6 shallots, thinly sliced

1 medium free-range egg

90 ml (3 fl oz) milk

85 g (3 oz) self-raising flour

25 g (1 oz) Parmesan, freshly grated

salt and pepper

a pinch of freshly grated nutmeg

tapenade

1 tbsp olive oil

3 garlic cloves, crushed or chopped

200 g (7 oz) pitted green olives

2 tsp grated lemon zest

2 tbsp balsamic vinegar

2 tbsp chopped flat-leaf parsley

garnish

1 tub of bocconcini
(mini mozzarella), sliced

salt and pepper

15 g (½ oz) fresh basil, cut into
julienne strips

1 tsp olive oil

1 To make the pancakes, melt the butter in a non-stick frying pan. Add the shallots and cook until golden. Whisk the egg and milk together, then add the shallots, flour, Parmesan, salt, pepper, and nutmeg, and mix.

2 Drop 4 separate tsp of the mixture into the butter in the frying pan. Cook for several minutes until golden brown on both sides and firm to the touch. Repeat until the batter is used up. Set aside until needed.

3 For the tapenade, preheat the olive oil in a frying pan and sauté the garlic until golden brown. Allow to cool, then place with all the remaining ingredients in a food processor. Pulse until chunky.

4 Marinate the sliced bocconcini cheeses with salt and pepper, basil, and olive oil.

5 To assemble, arrange the shallot pancakes on a serving plate and place ½ tsp of the tapenade on top. Garnish with a slice of marinated bocconcini.

diva**dos**

 Red onions can be used instead of shallots, but shallots are far sweeter. If bocconcini are not available, use chopped mozzarella. Rinse the olives in hot water before use to remove brine, then drain.

 The pancakes can be made a day ahead and reheated. The tapenade can be made several days ahead, covered and kept in a cool place.

 Use a good-quality non-stick frying pan. Be sure to brown the pancakes properly on both sides to cook out the floury flavour.

 The pancakes can be served cold and topped 1 hour before serving. If serving warm, heat through in the oven at 150°C/300°F/Gas 2 for 15 minutes. Top when out of the oven.

diva**don'ts**

 Don't use white onions, as they are too watery.

sun-blush tomato pesto with pitta breadsticks

● Makes 24 canapés to serve 10 ● Preparation: 20 minutes ● Cooking: 15 minutes

Long pitta crisps are dipped in a piquant dip of sun-blush tomatoes, harissa and Parmesan. Perfect as a sophisticated canapé or a casual dip.

pesto

250 g (9 oz) sun-blush tomatoes, drained of oil (sun-dried tomatoes in oil can be substituted)

175 g (6 oz) Parmesan, freshly grated

125 g (4½ oz) pine kernels, toasted

1 garlic clove, peeled

2 tbsp harissa or other chilli paste

1 tsp each of salt and pepper

125 ml (4 fl oz) extra virgin olive oil

pitta breadsticks

2 garlic cloves, crushed

4 tbsp olive oil

6 large white pitta breads

2 tbsp thyme leaves

1½ tsp salt

1 tsp pepper

1 Combine all the pesto ingredients except for the oil in a food processor. Once chopped finely, slowly add the oil until it is combined. Taste for seasoning.

2 To start the pitta breadsticks, preheat the oven to 180°C/350°F/ Gas 4. Stir the garlic into the oil. Slice the pitta breads lengthways into long thin strips. Snip the end of each strip to separate the strips. Place the pitta

strips in a large roasting tray, drizzle the garlic oil over, and toss to coat evenly. Sprinkle with thyme, salt and pepper. Bake until crisp and golden brown, about 15 minutes, shaking the tray occasionally. Cool on a rack.

3 To serve, place the pesto in a bowl, and serve with baskets of the crispy pitta sticks.

diva**dos**

 Buy the sun-blush tomatoes from an Italian grocer, as they are superior in quality to those you can buy in the supermarkets. Harissa is available from most supermarkets, and it will keep for ages in your refrigerator. It's fantastic on just about everything.

 Make the pitta breadsticks up to 2 days ahead, but store them in an airtight container. Make the pesto up to 2 days ahead, and keep in the refrigerator.

 Make as a dip for more casual parties. Place breadsticks standing up in a large glass, with the pesto in a shallow bowl. Serve the dip with the home-made Diva Breadsticks (with garlic and rosemary confit or red onion and prosciutto) on page 158.

spiced chicken empanaditas with green chilli sauce

● Makes 20 canapés to serve 10 ● Preparation: 1 hour ● Cooking: 25 minutes

Attractive and extremely moreish, empanaditas get a party going!
Serve as a canapé, a finger food, or a starter.

pastry

175 g (6 oz) plain flour

25 g (1 oz) butter

a pinch of salt

sunflower oil for deep-frying

filling

1 tbsp sunflower oil

½ medium onion, finely chopped

3 garlic gloves, finely chopped

175 g (6 oz) chicken breast meat
(approx. 1 breast), minced

½ tsp dried chilli flakes

½ tsp ground cumin

¼ tsp ground cinnamon

a pinch of ground cloves

125 ml (4 fl oz) tomato juice

1 tsp tomato paste

10 pitted green olives, finely chopped

2 tbsp raisins

salt and pepper

green chilli sauce

1 ripe avocado, peeled,
stoned and chopped

2 green chillies, seeded

15 g (½ oz) fresh coriander

2 spring onions, chopped

1 tbsp olive oil

grated zest and juice of 1 lime

salt and pepper

1 garlic clove

1 For the green chilli sauce, place all the ingredients in a food processor and puree, then taste to check the seasoning. If your limes are dry, you may need to add more lime juice.

2 To make the pastry, place the flour, butter and salt in a food processor and pulse until the mixture resembles fine breadcrumbs. Add 90 ml (3 fl oz) warm water to make a soft dough. Roll out on a lightly floured work surface with a floured rolling pin. Using a 7.5 cm (3 in) cookie cutter, stamp out 20 rounds. Chill.

3 For the filling, heat the oil in a large frying pan and sauté the onion and garlic until softened. Add the chicken and stir to break up the lumps while the meat is browning. Add the chilli and spices, and stir until the chicken is cooked through. Add the tomato juice, paste, olives, and raisins, and season with salt and pepper. Taste to check the seasoning. Allow to cool before using.

4 To fill the empanaditas, place a tsp of the cold chicken mixture into the centre of each pastry round. Using a little water on your fingertips, fold the pastry over the filling to make a half-moon shape, and seal by pinching the edges together. Place the empanaditas in a single layer on a tray, and keep chilled until ready to deep-fry.

5 To cook, preheat the oil to 160°C/375°F. When hot, add 4 empanaditas at a time, and fry for 5 minutes. Drain well on kitchen paper and keep warm in a low oven.

6 To serve, pile on a serving plate, with the green chilli sauce in a dipping bowl.

diva**dos**

 Your butcher can mince the chicken, or mince it yourself by dicing and placing in the food processor to puree. Minced pork, white fish or prawns can be used instead of chicken.

 The pastry and filling can be made a day ahead, the sauce 6 hours ahead and the empanaditas filled and refrigerated 6 hours ahead.

diva**don'ts**

 Don't fill the empanaditas whilst the filling is still warm. Don't fry too many at once – the oil temperature will drop and the pastry will become soggy.

 Don't pile the uncooked empanaditas on top of each other, as they will stick.

warm roquefort wontons

● Makes 20 canapés to serve 10   ● Preparation: 45 minutes   ● Cooking: 10 minutes

Everyone loves to crunch into wontons with tasty fillings. This one will take your guests by surprise since we've combined the crispy wrapper with a delicious creamy cheese and herb filling.

40 wonton wrappers

sunflower oil for deep-frying

filling

125 g (4½ oz) ricotta cheese

100 g (3½ oz) Roquefort cheese

grated zest of ½ lemon

25 g (1 oz) basil leaves, chopped

3 spring onions, finely chopped

salt and pepper

a pinch of freshly grated nutmeg

1 Mash the wonton filling ingredients together with a large fork. Place in a bowl, cover and chill for at least 30 minutes.

2 Take 1 wonton wrapper, brush with a little water and place another wrapper on top. Spoon a small tsp of the mixture in the centre, then dampen the edges with a little water. Bring the edges up into the

shape of an old-fashioned purse or a traditional pasta tortellini. Repeat with the remaining wrappers and the mixture.

3 Heat the oil in a large pan to 190°C/375°F, or preheat a deep-fat fryer, and fry the wontons in batches of about 5 until golden. Keep warm in a medium hot oven until ready to serve.

diva**dos**

 Fresh thyme could replace the basil in the filling.

 The wontons can be filled 1 hour beforehand, then chilled in a single layer. The filling could be made the day ahead, covered and chilled.

 You could serve the wontons with a spicy roasted tomato dipping sauce. Arrange them on a large, brightly painted plate with wedges of lemon.

 The wontons can be fried and kept warm for an hour before serving.

diva**don'ts**

 Don't allow the filled wontons to become too warm before frying, as the cheese mixture will leak out. Don't use too much water when wrapping the wontons; you actually need very little.

mini caesar salads en croûte

● Makes 20 canapés to serve 10   ● Preparation: 30 minutes   ● Cooking: 10 minutes

Everyone loves Caesar salad. But what transforms this version from classic-yet-common to downright-Diva-delectable is its original miniature, stunning presentation.

croûtes and salad

7 pieces of thinly sliced white bread

3 tbsp olive oil

10 anchovies (fresh, canned in olive oil or salted, optional)

a little milk

1 little gem or heart of cos lettuce

20 Parmesan shavings

a handful of chives, chopped

Caesar dressing

2 egg yolks

1 tsp Dijon mustard

1 garlic clove, peeled

2 anchovy fillets (as above)

1 tbsp white wine vinegar

1 tsp caster sugar

salt and pepper

150 ml (5 fl oz) sunflower oil

15 g (½ oz) Parmesan, freshly grated

1 For the dressing, place the egg yolks, mustard, garlic, anchovies, vinegar, sugar, salt, and pepper in a food processor. Slowly drizzle in the oil while blending to form a thick, creamy dressing. Stir in the grated Parmesan.

2 For the croûtes, preheat the oven to 200°C/400°F/Gas 6. Place the bread slices on your work surface and remove the crusts. Flatten by rolling a heavy rolling pin over the bread several times. Using a square or round 5.5 cm (2¼ in) biscuit cutter, stamp out 3 croûtes per slice of bread, ending up with approximately 20 croûtes. Push each croûte into

a mini muffin tin. Brush the inside of each with olive oil and bake in the preheated oven for 8 minutes until golden brown. Check if they need another 2 minutes; it depends on the oven.

3 To assemble the salad, slice each anchovy in half lengthways and soak in a little milk. Drain and pat dry with kitchen paper. Slice the lettuce thinly and gently toss with the Caesar dressing. Place a tsp of salad into each croûte.

4 Garnish each with a Parmesan shaving, some chives and a slice of anchovy.

diva**dos**

 Make the croûtes well ahead and store in an airtight container.

 Soak anchovies in milk for up to 10 minutes to remove the strong fishy flavour so many people dislike.

 Go for all-out sophistication and garnish each croûte with a soft-boiled quail's egg.

diva**don'ts**

 Don't dress the salad more than an hour before serving. There is nothing more unpalatable than a soggy Caesar!

spiced corn cakes with avocado-lime salsa

● Makes 20 canapés to serve 10   ● Preparation: 35 minutes   ● Cooking: 10 minutes

These slightly spiced, colourful little corn cakes, combined with fresh avocado salsa, make a delectable combination.

corn cakes

3 tbsp medium cornmeal

55 g (2 oz) plain flour

sea salt

6 tsp baking powder

1 egg, beaten

5 tbsp milk

1 tbsp butter, melted

½ tsp dried chilli flakes

2 spring onions, finely chopped

125 g (4½ oz) sweetcorn kernels, fresh or canned

cayenne pepper

3 tbsp sunflower oil

avocado-lime salsa

1 avocado, peeled, stoned and finely diced

½ medium red onion, finely chopped

juice of 1 lime

1 tbsp olive oil

salt and pepper

a dash of Tabasco sauce

to serve

fresh coriander

1 To prepare the corn cakes, mix all the ingredients, except for the oil, together in a large bowl. Preheat 1 tbsp oil in a non-stick frying pan. To make the corn cakes, place about 5 separate tsp of the mixture in the frying pan. Flip them over after about a minute, until browned on both sides. Repeat with the remaining mixture, using more oil as required. Allow to cool.

2 To make the salsa, simply mix the salsa ingredients together, and taste for seasoning.

3 To assemble, top each corn cake with a tsp of avocado-lime salsa and a coriander leaf.

divados

 Fresh sweetcorn kernels, when in season, make a huge difference.

 Make the corn cakes a day ahead, but keep chilled in an airtight container. Bring back to room temperature to serve, or you can reheat them for 5 minutes in a hot oven.

 You could use a large griddle pan to cook the cakes. Use a fish slice along with a tsp to gently turn the cakes over.

 Serve on a bamboo mat or plate lined with a banana leaf.

divadon'ts

 Don't make the salsa too far in advance. Prepare a couple of hours before serving and cover tightly with clingfilm.

 Don't undercook the cakes, otherwise they will fall apart when picked up.

smoked trout on toasted walnut bread with parsley-caper salsa

● Makes 20 canapés to serve 10   ● Preparation: 20 minutes

This sensational combination of ingredients is easy to prepare – and pure elegance.

5 slices of walnut bread, toasted

55 g (2 oz) cream cheese

100 g (3½ oz) smoked trout, cut into strips

pepper

parsley-caper salsa

1 tbsp baby capers

15 g (½ oz) flat-leaf parsley, finely chopped

2 spring onions, finely chopped

1 tbsp olive oil

grated zest of ½ lemon

½ tsp Dijon mustard

1 To make the salsa, drain, rinse and dry the capers, then mix them with the chopped parsley, chopped spring onion, olive oil, lemon zest and mustard. Taste and adjust the seasoning accordingly.

2 Spread the cream cheese evenly over the toasted walnut bread and cut each piece of toast into 4 even pieces. You can use a shaped cookie cutter.

3 Arrange the smoked trout in a little mound on each piece of toast and pile a little spoonful of the salsa on top of the trout. Garnish with ground black pepper.

diva**dos**

 Smoked salmon can substitute for smoked trout. Try using other breads, such as rye, olive, or caraway. Finely chopped shallot can replace the spring onion.

 The bread can be toasted up to 4 hours ahead. The salsa can be prepared up to 6 hours ahead and kept covered and chilled.

 The salsa makes an excellent topping for crostini. You can also garnish with sprigs of fresh dill.

diva**don'ts**

 Don't assemble more than an hour in advance. Don't make the salsa too runny (some parsley has more water in it): the salsa should be spooning consistency.

smoked salmon in filo cups with roasted pepper and dill salsa

● Makes 20 canapés to serve 10   ● Preparation: 45 minutes   ● Cooking: 10 minutes

Delicate filo tartlets filled with a silky combination of salmon, roasted peppers, dill, and lime. A perfect complement for other Mediterranean courses.

filo tartlets

12 filo pastry sheets

25 g (1 oz) butter, melted

salmon and salsa filling

150 g (5 oz) smoked salmon, cut into slices

1 red pepper and 1 yellow pepper

4 tbsp extra virgin olive oil

1 tbsp balsamic vinegar

1 garlic clove, finely chopped

6 basil leaves, finely chopped

1 lime, peeled, segmented and halved

2 tbsp chopped dill

1 tsp each of salt and pepper

100 g (3½ oz) crème fraîche

1 To make the tartlets, preheat the oven to 180°C/350°F/Gas 4, and follow instruction 1 on page 37. Carefully remove the tartlets from the tins and cool on racks.

2 To make the filling, slice the salmon. Blacken the peppers under the grill until dark on all sides. Place in a bag and leave for 5 minutes. Remove from the bag, peel away skin and discard seeds and stems.

Cut the pepper flesh into small dice and place in a small bowl. Add the oil, vinegar, garlic, basil, halved lime segments, dill, salt, and pepper. Leave to marinate for at least an hour.

3 To assemble, place 1 tsp crème fraîche into each tartlet, place a swirl of salmon on top, top with 1 tsp of the pepper salsa, and garnish with extra dill or basil.

diva**dos**

 Be sure to use a good-quality smoked salmon – or you could substitute smoked trout.

 Make the salsa the night before and refrigerate. You can make the filo tartlets at least a week before and keep them in an airtight container.

 Try serving the salsa with a smoked salmon salad as a starter, along with rye or walnut bread.

diva**don'ts**

 Don't assemble the tartlets more than half an hour ahead as the pastry will go soggy.

garnishes

As much attention should be paid to food presentation as to its flavour. Some say it is the most important aspect of good cooking. We cannot completely agree with that statement. Imagine how disappointing it would be bite into a spectacular looking dish, only to be greeted by dull and uninteresting flavours.

CHILLIES

A vibrant garnish for canapés, salads, barbecued foods and oriental dishes. Choose long, not tiny or balloon-shaped, chillies, as the latter are too hot. Cut in half lengthways, and run a teaspoon down the inside to remove the seeds. Lay the chilli flat on a chopping board and, using a small serrated knife, slice into very thin julienne strips. Arrange 3-4 strips of julienne into the appropriate dishes. Keep, chilled and covered, for one day.

OVEN-DRIED CHERRY TOMATOES

Serve in salads, with hot vegetables, to garnish roasted meats and to top crostini. Cut in half, lay on a baking tray and drizzle with olive oil and balsamic vinegar, sprinkle with salt and pepper and roast for 30 minutes in the oven preheated to 180°C/350°F/ Gas 4. Cool and store in one layer in a plastic container.

PICKLED GINGER

Normally served with fresh sushi, this bright pink garnish can be bought from most supermarkets and oriental shops. It is an attractive decoration for most oriental foods, providing good flavour and vibrant colour. We slice it thinly and stack it on dishes such as canapés, noodle salads, salmon or Asian marinated fish. Keep pickled ginger in its jar in a cool place.

ROSEMARY SKEWERS

The rosemary flavour spreads through the skewered, usually barbecued, food. Choose long, firm rosemary stems. Pull off all the leaves, leaving half an inch of leaves at the tip of the stalk for garnish. Carve a sharp end to aid skewering the food. Prepare 2 days beforehand.

FRESH HERBS

Herbs provide a light, fresh way to garnish any dish. We recommend basil, flat-leaf parsley, dill, coriander, rosemary, thyme, chives, oregano, chervil and Thai basil. Chiffonade basil leaves by stacking 4 on top of each other. Roll up tightly and slice very thinly. Chop chives finely or into long diagonal pieces. Use whole coriander or flat-leaf parsley sprigs and leaves. Deep fry thyme sprigs and sage leaves to garnish winter warm salads, pastas and roasts. To keep fresh, store in a cool, moist, airy place.

SPRING ONION JULIENNE

Thinly julienned, these are incredibly versatile for oriental and Mediterranean dishes dishes. Trim and slice in half lengthways. Cut into thin julienne strips lengthways or diagonally into thin slices. If you require tiny curled julienne, place in iced water. Prepare a day ahead.

CITRUS FRUIT

Citrus fruits add flavour as well as colour. We use segments, grated zest or julienned rind.

Segmenting citrus fruits: Cut away the rind and pith. Slide a knife down one side of each segment, cutting it away from the skin. Cut down the other side and pull out the segment. Store in a sealed container for up to 2 days. Delicious with smoked fish, salads or desserts.

Cutting julienne strips: With a potato peeler, peel the rind off the fruit, leaving the pith behind. Or scrape the pith off the back of the rind with a serrated knife. Stack several strips on top of each other and cut them into very thin julienne. They can be served raw or you can blanch them in boiling water for 1 minute to soften. Store in a plastic container. Use on savoury or sweet dishes.

CUCUMBER CUPS AND RIBBONS

Cucumber cups: Light, fresh and elegant, use these for canapés with a variety of fillings (see pages 28–29). Store in one layer, covered and chilled for up to a day. Fill no more than one hour before serving.

Cucumber ribbons: Peel the cucumber with a vegetable peeler, and discard the skin. Run the peeler down the cucumber in order to create long, thin ribbons. Keep in the fridge for up to 4 hours. A good garnish for oriental dishes or to toss with other ingredients for a salad.

TOASTED SESAME SEEDS

We use these to give a light nutty crunch to many foods, especially canapés, noodle salads and Middle Eastern desserts. They are quick and easy to apply and will not soften like herbs do. You must be careful when toasting as they burn easily. Preheat the oven to 180°C/350°F/Gas 4. Scatter the seeds on to a flat baking tray and toast for 7 minutes until evenly browned. Alternatively, toast them in a frying pan over medium heat, stirring several times. They keep well in a sealed container.

PARMESAN SHAVINGS

Start with a large hunk of Parmesan. Use a potato peeler or a serrated knife, and peel away the cheese in long thin wafers. Carefully place on a plate and store in the fridge for several days. A great garnish for salads, soups, crostini or bruschetta.

JULIENNE OF GINGER

A useful garnish for oriental canapés, Asian meat dishes, poultry, soups and desserts. Choose really fresh ginger, with skin that is shiny and moist, not dry and hairy. Peel away the hard skin, and slice the flesh into thin, uniform strips. Pile the strips on top of each other and cut into julienne. They can be stored in a covered container, chilled, for several days.

CROSTINI/TOASTED BREADS

Crostini should be made from the thinnest French bread sticks you can buy. A day old bread stick works best. Slice the bread into 1cm (½in) discs, brush with olive oil, sprinkle with sea salt, and lay on a baking tray. Place in an oven preheated to 180°C/350°F/Gas 4 for 10 minutes until lightly golden and crisp. Make up to 2 weeks in advance and store in an airtight container. Serve plain, topped or with salads and soups.

JAPANESE SESAME SEEDS

Buy these already mixed in bottles from supermarkets and oriental shops. 'Japanese Seasoning' includes white and black sesame seeds, Nori seaweed and red shiso leaves. This provides a delicious, nutty, slightly salty and colourful garnish.

sri lankan fish cakes with tomato sambal

● Makes 20 canapés to serve 10   ● Preparation: 45 minutes   ● Cooking: 20 minutes

After a wonderful visit to Sri Lanka, there were many culinary inspirations that came home. This recipe is adapted from the fish cakes made for us daily by a very gifted cook we luckily met during our stay.

2 tbsp vegetable oil

150 g (5½ oz) cooked flaked fish
(tuna, haddock or cod)

2 shallots, finely chopped

175 g (6 oz) mashed cooked potato

1 green chilli, chopped
(more if you prefer spicy food)

4 curry leaves, chopped

salt and pepper

a good pinch of cayenne pepper

grated zest and juice of 1 lime

2 eggs, beaten

55 g (2 oz) fine fresh breadcrumbs

sunflower oil for deep-frying

tomato sambal

6 ripe tomatoes

1 red onion, finely diced

1 green chilli, finely chopped

juice of 1 lemon

1 tbsp olive oil

salt and pepper

1 To start the sambal, skin and seed the tomatoes. Cut an X at the bottom of each and dip into a pan of boiling water until the skin starts to peel back. Immediately place the tomatoes in a bowl of cold water and slip off the loose skin. Cut the tomatoes in half and scoop out the seeds. Finely chop the tomato flesh and add the red onion, green chilli, lemon juice, olive oil and some salt and pepper. Set aside until needed.

2 To make the fish cakes, heat the oil in a large saucepan and add all the fish cake ingredients, except for the lime zest and juice, eggs, breadcrumbs and sunflower oil.

Cook over a medium heat for a few minutes. Mash the ingredients together with a large wooden spoon. Add the lime zest and juice, and taste for additional seasoning. Form little balls and roll in egg and then breadcrumbs. Chill until needed.

3 To cook, preheat deep-fat fryer or a pan with the oil, and fry 5 cakes at a time until golden. Drain well on kitchen paper, and keep warm in a medium oven until all are made. Serve warm with the tomato sambal.

diva**dos**

 Fresh coriander could be added to the fish cakes for variety.

 The fish cakes can be made the day before, as can the tomato sambal. Chill and cover.

 Serve sprinkled with sea salt and large wedges of fresh lime.

diva**don'ts**

 Don't add the seasoning and lemon juice to the sambal until 1 hour before serving.

 Don't seed the chilli as this is the true Sri Lankan flavour. If you fear it will be too hot, use less large chillies. Although the smaller the chilli, the hotter...

asian gravadlax on star toast with chilli crème fraîche

● Makes 25 canapés to serve 10–12   ● Preparation: 3 days' marinating and 30 minutes

Making your own gravadlax couldn't be easier and more elegant. Once the fish has marinated, you simply slice and serve.

salmon

2 tbsp caster sugar

2 tbsp salt

500 g (1 lb 2 oz) salmon fillet with skin (1 centre-cut piece)

2.5 cm (1 in) piece of fresh root ginger, peeled and grated

1 lemongrass stalk, lower parts only, hard layers removed, finely chopped

grated rind of 1 lime

½ tsp coriander seeds, toasted and ground

1 tsp pepper

1 red chilli, seeded and finely chopped

3 tbsp finely chopped fresh coriander

1 tbsp finely chopped mint

chilli crème fraîche

200 ml (7 fl oz) crème fraîche

1 tbsp finely chopped mint

2 small red chillies, seeded and finely diced

juice of 1 lime

2 tbsp chopped fresh coriander

salt and pepper

to serve

12–14 pieces white bread

1 small cucumber, seeded and finely diced

fresh coriander leaves

julienne strips of seeded red chilli

1 For the gravadlax, combine the sugar and salt and rub into both sides of the salmon. Mix the remaining salmon ingredients together and paste all over the fish. Wrap tightly in clingfilm. Place on a small cutting board and top with another board. Weight down with heavy tins or weights, and leave in the refrigerator for 3 days, turning the gravadlax over twice.

2 When the salmon has cured, remove the wrapping, and wipe off excess marinade. Place on a wooden board and use a sharp, long narrow knife to slice. Hold the knife almost parallel to the fish and slice 3 mm (⅛ in) thick.

3 For the chilli crème fraîche, mix all the ingredients together, seasoning to taste, and refrigerate.

4 For the toasts, preheat the oven to 200°C/400°F/Gas 6. Using a star-shaped biscuit cutter, cut out 2 stars from each slice. Place on a baking sheet and bake for 8 minutes, turning the toasts over once.

5 To assemble, top each toast with 1 tsp chilli crème fraîche, and curl a slice of salmon around on the top. Garnish with cucumber, a coriander leaf and chilli julienne.

diva**dos**

 Check the salmon for any remaining bones, and remove with tweezers. You could substitute the salmon with a more glamorous fish like tuna.

 Make the chilli crème fraîche and star toasts the day before, but keep the toasts in an airtight container.

 Serve on its own for a starter or impressive brunch dish.

diva**don'ts**

 Don't slice the salmon until the day of the party, and remember to sharpen your knife beforehand.

prawn, mint and ginger spring rolls

● Makes 25 canapés to serve 10 –12   ● Preparation: 1 hour

Unlike their deep-fried cousins from China, Thai spring rolls are made from a rice paper wrapper that's soaked in water before rolling. The result is a fresh healthy snack that is full of South-East Asian flavours. Serve with a peanut dipping sauce.

250 g (9 oz) medium cooked, peeled prawns

2 medium red onions, thinly sliced

2 large carrots, cut into julienne strips

1 x 10 cm (4 in) piece of daikon or white radish, cut into julienne strips (optional)

1 x 7.5 cm (3 in) piece fresh root ginger, cut into julienne strips

12 fresh coriander sprigs, about 7.5 cm (3 in) long

24 Thai basil leaves (ordinary basil will do as well)

24 mint leaves

12 circular rice paper wrappers (15 cm (6 in) in diameter)

peanut dipping sauce

1 tsp vegetable oil

1½ tsp chopped garlic

1 tsp dried red chilli flakes or chilli bean paste

60 ml (2 fl oz) hoisin sauce

2 tbsp smooth peanut butter

1 tsp tomato puree

1 tsp caster sugar

75 ml (2½ fl oz) water

1 Place the prawns, onion, carrots, white radish, and ginger in separate piles on a plate. Set out the fresh herbs in small stacks.

2 Place a large tea-towel on your work surface. Pour hot water into a bowl. Drop one rice paper wrapper at a time into the water for about 30 seconds. When soft and pliable, place the wrapper on the tea-towel and wipe off excess water with another towel.

3 Place 2 mint leaves on the top portion of the wrapper. Place 4 prawns across the diameter of the circle. Make sure they are at the lower part of the wrapper. Place a small amount of the onion, carrot, white radish and ginger, a coriander sprig and 2 basil leaves over the prawns. Bring up the lower front of the rice paper over the vegetables and then fold the sides in. Roll up the front side until it is a tight spring roll. Place seam-side down on a tea-towel. When rolling up, try and make it as tight as possible without ripping the

wrapper. Throw away any wrapper that rips and start again with a fresh one. It may take a few to get the knack, so don't be discouraged. If the wrapper is too soft, it will fall apart, and if it's too hard, it will not stick together. Practise a few so you can get a feel for the right consistency.

4 When ready to serve, cut each spring roll in half diagonally with a very sharp knife. Place on a plate with a sushi mat, which makes an attractive presentation, or on a platter scattered with extra fresh coriander and mint leaves. Pour the peanut dipping sauce into a small bowl and serve on the side.

peanut dipping sauce

1 Heat the oil in a small saucepan until hot. Add the garlic and chilli and stir for 5 seconds.

2 Pour the mixture into a small bowl with the rest of the ingredients, and stir until smooth.

diva**dos**
Try Thai grocers for rice paper wrappers and Thai basil, or look carefully in your local supermarket.

diva**don'ts**
Don't make the spring rolls more than 6 hours in advance.

crispy crab and cream cheese wontons

● Makes 20 canapés to serve 10 ● Preparation: 25 minutes ● Cooking: 10 minutes

Crispy wontons with creamy hot cheese and crab are dipped into a sweet chilli sauce. It's pure decadence!

175 g (6 oz) fresh or canned crab meat – white meat only!

200 g (7 oz) cream cheese

2 spring onions, thinly sliced

1 small red chilli, seeded and diced

salt and pepper

40 wonton wrappers

1 egg white

vegetable oil for deep-frying

Thai sweet chilli sauce

1 Mix the crab, cream cheese, spring onions, chilli, salt, and pepper in a small mixing bowl.

2 Place half the wonton wrappers on a clean tea towel with the corners facing towards you. Brush each wonton with egg white. Place a second wonton on top of the brushed wonton, creating a double thickness. Place a tsp of the crab filling in the lowest corner. Brush egg white around all sides of the wrapper. Fold the wrapper over the filling. It should look like a triangle at this point. Take

the top 2 corners of the wrapper and pinch together into a tortellini shape. Brush with more egg white to seal if needed. Repeat with the remaining wontons.

3 Heat the oil in a large heavy pot to 190°C/375°F, or until a small piece of bread sizzles instantly. Fry 5 wontons at a time until crisp, then drain well on kitchen paper.

4 Serve immediately with the Thai dipping sauce.

diva**dos**

 Buy a large bottle of Thai sweet chilli sauce from your Asian grocer. It keeps for ages and it's delicious on anything fried. You can replace the crab meat with chopped cooked prawns.

 The wontons can be deep-fried ahead and reheated in the oven at 200°C/400°F/Gas 6 for 5 minutes to crisp.

diva**don'ts**

 Ensure the oil is hot enough, otherwise the wontons will be greasy and soggy. Use a deep-fat fryer if possible, or a thick-based heavy saucepan. These will maintain the heat level of the oil far better.

spicy prawns with moroccan tomato jam

● Makes 24 canapés to serve 12   ● Preparation: 10 minutes   ● Cooking: 1 hour

Large juicy prawns are grilled with a gorgeous spicy tomato jam. The perfect food to start an exotic evening. You will need 24 wooden skewers, which you should soak in water for an hour before using.

24 king-size prawns, peeled and deveined

24 x 5 cm (2 in) pieces of spring onion

1 tbsp clear honey

a small handful of fresh coriander, chopped

moroccan tomato jam

2 garlic cloves, finely chopped

2 tbsp finely chopped fresh root ginger

2 tbsp olive oil

125 ml (4 fl oz) cider vinegar

1 cinnamon stick

2 x 400 g (14 oz) cans peeled plum tomatoes, chopped or pureed

4 tbsp soft brown sugar

1 tsp ground cumin

½ tsp cayenne pepper

⅛ tsp ground cloves

salt and pepper

1 Sauté the garlic and ginger in the olive oil for 2 minutes. Add the vinegar and cinnamon stick, and cook for 1 minute. Stir in the remaining ingredients. Reduce the heat and cook gently until all the liquid has evaporated, about 1 hour. Keep an eye on it to prevent burning. Remove the cinnamon. Allow to cool to room temperature.

2 Preheat a grill or barbecue. Coat the prawns with tomato jam and place one on each skewer with a piece of spring onion. Drizzle the honey over, and grill for 1 minute each side.

3 Sprinkle with the chopped coriander, and serve with the remaining jam.

diva**dos**

 Buy canned tomatoes from a good Italian shop, as the quality and colour are significantly better.

 Make the jam up to a week ahead, and refrigerate. Skewer the prawns in the morning and chill.

 Make a statement and arrange the skewers standing up on the platter, resting on the prawn. Serve with dishes like Filo Tart with Charmoula Chicken or Couscous with Roasted Sweet Potato (see pages 52 and 105).

diva**don'ts**

 Don't forget to soak the skewers, otherwise they will catch light and you will have a small bonfire under your grill!

cucumber cups with thai prawns

● Makes 20 canapés to serve 10   ● Preparation: 30 minutes

This is the fastest canapé you can possibly make. These little cucumber cups can be used with all kinds of delectable fillings, but we think the prawns with chilli sauce is the best.

2 large, long cucumbers

125 g (4½ oz) cooked and shelled medium prawns

15 g (½ oz) fresh coriander, chopped

6 tbsp Thai sweet chilli sauce

toasted sesame seeds to garnish (optional)

1 To make the cucumber cups, cut the cucumbers into 20 x 5 cm (2 in) thick slices. Stamp each slice with a suitably sized crinkled pastry cutter, removing the cucumber skin. Using a melon baller or teaspoon, make a hollow in the centre of the cucumber cups to nestle your filling in.

2 Drain and pat the prawns dry. Place in a bowl with the chopped coriander and chilli sauce, and mix well.

3 Fill each cucumber cup with chilli prawns, and scatter toasted sesame seeds (if using) on top.

diva**dos**

 A mousse made from blue cheese, mixed well with cream cheese, is delicious in these cups, topped with crispy bacon and chives. Or you could try thin slices of smoked salmon with pickled ginger and wasabi.

 The cucumber cups can be made the day before. Chill, covered, on kitchen paper. The prawn filling can be mixed together 1 hour before serving.

 The cucumber cups are great with any fried foods, as these create such a texture contrast.

diva**don'ts**

 Don't fill the cucumber cups with prawns more than 30 minutes before serving.

indian pakoras with two dipping sauces

- Makes 25 canapés to serve 10–12   • Preparation: 45 minutes   • Cooking: 15 minutes

Pakoras are the tempura of India – deep-fried vegetable slices in a spicy batter. They are irresistible with these two dipping sauces.

25 slices of any of these vegetables: onion, potato, baby or small aubergine, baby artichoke, green beans or fennel

vegetable oil for deep-frying

batter

25 g (1 oz) gram flour (chickpea flour)

45 g (1½ oz) self-raising flour

½ tsp garam masala

½ tsp ground cumin

½ tsp ground turmeric

½ tsp chilli powder

½ tsp salt

coriander and mint dipping sauce

250 g (9 oz) Greek yogurt

1 shallot, finely chopped

1 tbsp finely grated fresh ginger root

2 small mild green chillies, seeded and chopped

1 tbsp caster sugar

20 mint leaves

25 g (1 oz) fresh coriander

salt and pepper

tamarind dipping sauce

2 tbsp dried tamarind pulp, or 150 g (5 oz) bottled puree

2 tbsp soft brown sugar

½ tsp each of ground cumin, ground fennel seeds, finely grated fresh root ginger and salt

1 tsp lemon juice

1 For the batter, combine the flours, spices and salt with 150 ml (5 fl oz) water and beat to a smooth batter. The batter should be thick, so add additional flour if necessary.

2 Heat the oil to 190°C/375°F, or until a piece of bread sizzles instantly.

3 Peel the onion, keeping the root end on. Cut in thin slices lengthways so there is a bit of root left to hold the layers together. Aubergine should be left unpeeled and sliced thinly. Artichoke should have hard leaves and stems removed and then be sliced thinly. Remove outer leaves from the fennel and slice out the core – slice thinly. Green beans should be topped and tailed, and left whole.

4 Dip the pieces of vegetable one at a time into the batter, and then drop into the hot oil. Fry up to 6 pieces at a time. Drain on kitchen paper.

5 Serve immediately with dipping sauces in bowls on the side.

coriander and mint dipping sauce

Place all the ingredients in a food processor and process until smooth. Season to taste.

tamarind dipping sauce

1 Place the tamarind pulp in a bowl and cover with 125 ml/4 fl oz hot water. Leave to soak until the water cools. Squeeze the pulp until thoroughly dissolved in the water. Strain through a mesh sieve, pushing all the pulp through, and adding a little more water if necessary. Discard the fibres and seeds. If using the bottled tamarind puree, then mix with 3 tbsp water.

2 Add the remaining ingredients to the tamarind, and stir well.

diva**dos**

Visit your local Indian food shop, which will be an Aladdin's cave of spices and other interesting ingredients. Use baby vegetables when you can find them, which look very glamorous.

Make the pakoras 3 hours ahead and then reheat in the oven at 200°C/400°F/Gas 6 for

5 minutes. (This also gives you time to remove the frying odour from your kitchen.) The tamarind dipping sauce can be made a week before, and kept cool. Make the other sauce just before serving.

diva**don'ts**

Don't slice the vegetables too thick as they will not deep-fry properly.

wonton cups with chinese chicken salad

● Makes 20 canapés to serve 10   ● Preparation: 45 minutes   ● Cooking: 20 minutes

Light, refreshing, and tasty, these wonton cups make an impressive canapé for any occasion.

40 wonton wrappers

groundnut oil

Chinese chicken salad

1 boneless, skinless chicken breast

2 tbsp light soy sauce

1 tbsp rice vinegar

1 tbsp sesame oil

1 bunch spring onions, finely chopped

15 g (½ oz) flat-leaf parsley or fresh coriander, finely chopped

1 To start the wonton cups, preheat the oven to 180°C/350°F/Gas 4. Lay the wrappers out and very lightly brush them with oil. (If you have an oil spray bottle, that is better.) Stack 2 wrappers on top of each other at alternate angles and push into mini muffin tins. Bake the cups in the preheated oven for 8 minutes to crisp. Remove from the oven, cool and store until needed.

2 To make the filling, place the chicken breast in a pan of cold water, cover, bring to a simmer and cook

for 8 minutes. Turn off the heat, and allow the chicken to cool in the liquid.

3 Slice the chicken very thinly and mix with the soy, rice vinegar, sesame oil, spring onions, and parsley or coriander. Taste to check the flavour. Add more soy or vinegar if needed.

4 Fill each crisp wonton cup with the Chinese chicken salad, and serve at room temperature.

diva**dos**

 Use good-quality, free-range chicken for the salad.

 The wonton cups can be made 2 days beforehand, and stored in an airtight container. The chicken salad can be cooked the day before, covered and chilled, but don't add the liquid ingredients until 1 hour before serving.

 If cooking a larger number of chicken breasts, place in a water-filled roasting tin, cover with foil and cook at 180°C/350°F/Gas4 for 20 minutes. Poaching the chicken keeps it moist, which is the best method for this recipe.

 Garnish with toasted sesame seeds or red chilli, seeded and cut into julienne strips.

diva**don'ts**

 Don't fill the wonton cups with chicken salad until half an hour before serving.

tuna ceviche on corn tortillas with mango salsa

● Makes 24 canapés to serve 12   ● Preparation: 30–60 minutes   ● Cooking: 10 minutes

A perfect and elegant bite for a Latin evening. Lime-marinated tuna mixed with mango salsa is divine when paired with a warm crunchy tortilla. Don't forget the margaritas!

250 g (9 oz) fresh tuna, cut into small dice

125 ml (4 fl oz) fresh lime juice

vegetable oil for deep-frying

1 packet of 8 corn tortillas, each cut into 3 large wedge pieces

fresh coriander leaves

mango salsa

1 small fresh red chilli, seeded and chopped, or 1 chipotle pepper in adobo sauce, finely chopped

1 small red onion, finely chopped

1 tsp freshly cracked black pepper

1 tsp tequila

1 tsp salt

a small handful of fresh coriander (about 20 g (¾ oz), chopped

1 large ripe mango, peeled, stoned and finely diced

juice of 2 limes

1 Place the tuna in the lime juice and marinate for 30–60 minutes. Drain and mix thoroughly with all the salsa ingredients.

2 Heat the vegetable oil in a large frying pan. Prepare a bowl lined with kitchen paper. Test the oil: if hot enough, a small piece of tortilla will crisp and bubble very quickly. This is important as otherwise the tortillas will turn greasy when cooked. The

chips will cook quickly, so be prepared to remove after 30 seconds with a mesh spoon. Drain well on the kitchen paper. Alternatively, you can spray the corn tortillas with oil and bake in the oven at 200°C/400°F/Gas 6 for 8 minutes.

3 To serve, spoon 1 tbsp of ceviche salsa on to an individual tortilla chip, and place on a plate garnished with fresh coriander.

diva**dos**

 Use extremely good-quality tuna that is ruby red with very little fat marbling. Or use sea bass as an alternative. Select a large mango that is ripe but not mushy. If corn tortillas are not available, you can buy packaged corn tortilla chips.

 The mango salsa can be prepared 2 hours before serving, but don't add the lime juice until just before you are ready to serve.

 Serve the ceviche in a bowl with a basket of tortilla chips for a more casual setting.

diva**don'ts**

 Don't marinate the tuna for over an hour or the fish will become rubbery. Don't mix the tuna with the salsa until an hour before serving, as mango becomes slimy when left too long with lime juice.

gingered chicken cakes with coriander sauce

● Makes 20 canapés to serve 10 ● Preparation: 25 minutes ● Cooking: 20 minutes

We stumbled upon this recipe when Thai fish cakes had had their day in every menu and cookbook. This simple recipe is packed full of Oriental flavours, and works well as a canapé or, made larger, as a starter or main course.

gingered chicken cakes

2 boneless, skinless chicken breasts, chopped

3 tbsp Thai fish sauce (nam pla)

2.5 cm (1 in) fresh root ginger, peeled

3 spring onions, chopped

1 garlic clove, chopped

½ tsp sea salt

½ tsp dried chilli flakes

sunflower oil for shallow-frying

coriander sauce

2 tbsp classic Mayonnaise (see page 118)

15 g (½ oz) fresh coriander, finely chopped

juice and finely grated zest of 1 lime

1 To make the coriander sauce, mix the mayonnaise with the coriander, lime juice and zest. Cover and chill until needed.

2 For the gingered chicken cakes, place all the chicken cake ingredients except for the oil in a food processor, and puree until well combined. Scoop the mixture out into a bowl and shape into 20 small round cakes.

3 Heat 2.5 cm (1 in) sunflower oil in a large frying pan and brown the cakes for 3 minutes on both sides. Drain on kitchen paper.

4 Place on an oven tray and keep warm in a medium hot oven until ready to eat. Serve with a bowl of the coriander sauce.

diva**dos**

 Use really fresh ginger, otherwise it will go stringy in the food processor and be unpleasant to eat. Make sure the ginger is well chopped before combining with the chicken.

 The cakes can be made the day before and stored raw, covered, in the fridge. The sauce can keep, covered, for 1 week in the fridge. When shaping the cakes, it helps to have a small bowl of warm water available to dip your fingers in as it is quite a sticky job!

 If making the cakes in large numbers, you could brown them in the pan and cook through in a hotter oven to save time.

 Thai sweet chilli sauce also makes an excellent dip for these little cakes. Serve the cakes on a bamboo mat placed on a white plate. Add a small dipping bowl for the sauce, and garnish with wedges of lime.

diva**don'ts**

 Don't overcook the chicken cakes or they will become tough.

vietnamese grilled pork in lettuce parcels

● Makes 24 canapés to serve 12   ● Preparation: 45 minutes   ● Cooking: 15 minutes

These grilled, caramelised balls of minced pork contain all the great Vietnamese flavours. They're delicious served in crunchy lettuce parcels with a chilli sauce.

500 g (1 lb 2 oz) minced lean pork

4 shallots, finely chopped

3 garlic cloves, crushed

2 tbsp trimmed and finely chopped fresh lemongrass

1½ tsp cornflour

1 tbsp finely chopped mint

3 tbsp finely chopped fresh coriander

4 tbsp Thai fish sauce (nam pla)

½ tsp each of salt and pepper

55 g (2 oz) caster sugar

to serve

24 little gem or cos lettuce heart leaves, washed and dried

1 medium cucumber, peeled, seeded and diced

1 red onion, finely diced

mint and fresh coriander sprigs

Thai sweet chilli sauce

1 In a large bowl, mix together the pork, shallots, garlic, lemongrass, cornflour, mint, coriander, fish sauce, salt, and pepper.

2 Preheat the oven to 200°C/ 400°F/Gas 6.

3 With lightly oiled hands, shape the pork mixture into 24 x 4–5 cm (1½–2 in) balls. (They will shrink while cooking.) Roll each meatball in the sugar, and place on a baking tray lined with a sheet of greaseproof paper.

4 Bake in the preheated oven for 15 minutes. Shake the tray a couple of times while they cook, so that they don't burn on one side.

5 To serve, place a meatball on a lettuce leaf. Add some diced cucumber, onion, and a sprig of mint and coriander. Drizzle 1 tsp of sweet chilli sauce over each.

diva**dos**

 Get your pork from a butcher to ensure that it is of good quality and lean. He could mince it for you.

 You can prepare the pork balls 3–4 hours in advance. Before serving, reheat in the oven at 200°C/400°F/Gas 6 for 5 minutes until hot.

 Remember when using lemongrass to use the bottom third of the stalk. Smash with the flat side of a knife, and peel off the hard layers. Finely chop the soft piece left.

filo tartlets with seared duck and tomato-sesame chutney

● Makes 20 canapés to serve 10   ● Preparation: 1 hour   ● Cooking: 1 hour

A sumptuous meal made miniature. Tender pieces of duck set against a sweet and sour chutney make for pure heaven.

filo tartlets

12 filo pastry sheets

25 g (1 oz) butter, melted

duck filling

2 Barbary duck breasts

1 tbsp light soy sauce

1 tsp clear honey

tomato-sesame chutney

250 g (9 oz) ripe tomatoes

90 ml (3 fl oz) white wine vinegar

85 g (3 oz) caster sugar

a few fennel seeds

½ tsp curry powder

2 cardamom pods, split

a pinch each of cayenne pepper and ground ginger

a small handful of raisins

1 tbsp sesame seeds, toasted

1 Preheat the oven to 180°C/ 350°F/Gas 4. Brush 1 filo pastry sheet with some of the melted butter. Use a sharp knife to cut the pastry into 5 cm/2 in squares. Stack 4 squares at different angles on top of each other, so that the finished stack has a star-like appearance. Push the pastry firmly into a mini muffin tin to obtain a flat bottom for the tartlets. Repeat this process with the remaining pastry. Bake in the preheated oven for 6–8 minutes until golden. Carefully remove from the tins and cool on racks.

2 To start the chutney, skin the tomatoes by cutting an X in the bottom of each. Drop into a pan of boiling water for a minute, then place in a bowl of cold water to refresh for 1 minute before slipping off the skins. Roughly chop the tomatoes.

3 Heat the vinegar and sugar together over a low heat, stirring with

a wooden spoon until the sugar has dissolved. Raise the heat and add all the remaining ingredients except for the sesame seeds. Simmer for approximately 30 minutes until thickened. Cool and remove the cardamom pods. Set aside until needed.

4 Preheat the oven to 200°C/ 400°F/Gas 6. To prepare the duck, remove the fat if preferred, using a sharp knife to pull it away from the flesh. Brush the duck with the soy sauce and honey. Preheat a frying pan, and sear the duck breast – without any oil – for 2 minutes on each side, then roast in the preheated oven for 10 minutes until still pink. Rest and cool.

5 To assemble, slice the duck breasts thinly, and place 2 slices in each tartlet. Top with a tsp chutney, and scatter with toasted sesame seeds.

diva**dos**

Make the tomato-sesame chutney days or weeks in advance. It goes well with many meat and cheese dishes – it's quite valuable for daily Diva cooking. The filo tartlets can be made a week ahead and kept in an airtight container. The duck can be cooked the day before.

diva**don'ts**

You can garnish the tartlets with thinly sliced red chilli, coriander leaves or chives.

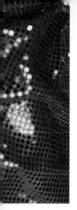

diva**tarts**

parsley and roasted garlic tart

● Serves: 8   ● Preparation: 1 hour   ● Cooking: 45 minutes

Any excuse to use roasted garlic will do. You may have guessed that we like it in just about anything!

1x 20 cm (8 in) blind-baked Herb Pastry case, made with flat-leaf parsley (see page 48)

olive oil

balsamic vinegar

salt and pepper

filling

3 garlic bulbs

250 g (9 oz) crème fraîche

4 medium eggs

juice and finely grated rind of 1 lemon

15 g (½ oz) chives

1 bunch of spring onions, washed and trimmed

55 g (2 oz) flat-leaf parsley, chopped

10 cherry plum tomatoes, halved

1 Preheat the oven to 180°C/ 350°F/Gas 4. Place the garlic bulbs on a large piece of foil, drizzle on a little olive oil and tightly seal the foil. Roast for 1 hour. Remove from the oven, open the foil up and allow to cool. Slice the garlic in half and squeeze all the roasted garlic pulp out. Discard the skins.

2 Place the garlic with all the remaining filling ingredients except for the tomatoes in a food processor. Puree. Pour the filling into the tart shell, and arrange the cherry tomato halves on top.

3 Drizzle with olive oil and balsamic vinegar, sprinkle with salt and pepper, and bake in the oven at the same temperature for 45 minutes.

diva**dos**

Basil also works well in this recipe.

The tart can be made a day ahead, and then warmed through to serve.

Puree the filling ingredients well, so that the mixture is bright green.

The recipe can be made into 8 individual tarts. Serve with Tuscan Panzanella Salad or a lovely Baby Green Salad with a tart vinaigrette (see pages 123 and 135).

diva**don'ts**

Don't allow the roasted garlic to get cold; it must be squeezed out while still warm.

caramelised red onion and fennel tarte tatin with olives and thyme

● Serves: 8 ● Preparation: 1 hour ● Cooking: 40 minutes

Roasted red onion and fennel, perched in flaky puff pastry with a balsamic caramel, is divine for a picnic or a winter dinner.

200 g (7 oz) puff pastry

filling

6 medium red onions, sliced into thick rings

3 fennel bulbs, halved, cored and cut into 6 pieces

2 tbsp olive oil

2 tbsp balsamic vinegar

2 garlic cloves, finely chopped

salt and pepper

55 g (2 oz) caster sugar

2 tbsp water

2 tsp chopped thyme

8 olives, pitted and halved

115 g (4 oz) Parmesan, freshly grated

1 Roll out the puff pastry on a floured surface to fit a 28 cm (11 in) tart tin. Place the rolled pastry on a plate and refrigerate for 30 minutes. Line the tart tin with greaseproof paper. (If using a heavy cake tin or tarte tatin pan, you won't need the paper.)

2 Meanwhile, preheat the oven to 180°C/350°F/Gas 4. Place the red onions and fennel in a shallow roasting pan. Pour over the olive oil and vinegar, and sprinkle with garlic, salt and pepper. Try and keep the onion ring slices intact. Bake for 30 minutes, carefully turning over once during cooking. Set aside to cool.

3 Combine the sugar with the water in a saucepan and stir over a low heat

until the sugar dissolves. Bring to the boil and cook, without stirring, until golden. Pour into the base of the prepared tin.

4 Firmly pack the onion slices, thyme and olives into the base of the prepared tin. Place the fennel pieces on top and sprinkle with Parmesan. Place the rolled pastry over the filling, and tuck the edges in to fit. Use a fork to prick tiny holes in the pastry to let the steam out.

5 Bake in the oven at the same temperature for 30–40 minutes until the pastry is puffed and golden. Let the tart cool for 5 minutes before turning out. Run a knife around the edge of the tart, then invert on to a warm plate.

diva**dos**

 You could ask your local pâtisserie or bakery if they will sell you some of their puff pastry; this will be a step up from the supermarket variety, or try making your own.

 Prepare the tart the day before, which enhances the flavours and eases turning out.

 If you double the recipe, then make 2 separate 28 cm (11 in) tarts.

 Indulge in a cast-iron, enamelled tarte tatin pan if your budget is up to it.

diva**don'ts**

 Don't stir the caramel while cooking or it will crystallise. Just skae the pan slightly and leave it to boil on its own – but watch carefully!

wild mushroom and smoked mozzarella tart

● Serves: 8   ● Preparation: 1 hour   ● Cooking: 45 minutes

Rich wild mushrooms are set with smoky mozzarella, Parmesan and a crisp olive crust for the perfect cold-weather tart.

fresh herb and olive pastry

200 g (7 oz) plain flour

100 g (3½ oz) salted butter, chilled and diced

15 g (½ oz) flat-leaf parsley, basil, oregano or thyme, finely chopped

1 tbsp black olive paste

1 medium egg

mushroom filling

25 g (1 oz) dried porcini mushrooms

2 tbsp olive oil

1 large Spanish onion, thinly sliced

2 garlic cloves, chopped

500 g (1 lb 2 oz) large dark field mushrooms, sliced

4 medium eggs

300 ml (10 fl oz) double cream

25 g (1 oz) flat-leaf parsley, chopped

25 g (1 oz) basil, torn (optional)

salt and pepper

freshly grated nutmeg, to taste

115 g (4 oz) smoked mozzarella, grated or chopped

115 g (4 oz) Parmesan, freshly grated

1 To make the pastry, we recommend using a food processor! Pulse the flour, butter, and chosen herb until the mixture resembles breadcrumbs. Add the black olive paste and egg, and puree until the pastry forms a ball. Place on a floured surface and roll out to line a 20 cm (8 in) loose-bottomed tart tin. Chill until required, at least 30 minutes.

2 Preheat the oven to 180°C/350°F/Gas 4. Blind-bake the tart shell (see page 48) for 10 minutes. Remove the paper and beans and allow to cool for 5 minutes before filling.

3 To make the mushroom filling, soak the dried mushrooms in 300 ml (10 fl oz) boiling water for about 20 minutes. Drain through a thin piece of cloth to ensure that all dirt and grit is

collected, reserving the liquid. Rinse the dried mushrooms and chop coarsely.

4 Meanwhile, heat the olive oil in a large pan and sauté the onion and garlic until soft. Add the sliced field mushrooms and cook gently for 10 minutes. Add the chopped dried mushrooms with 125 ml (4 fl oz) of the reserved liquid. Remove from the heat.

5 Meanwhile, preheat the oven to 190°C/375°F/Gas 5.

6 In a large bowl, beat together the eggs, cream, herbs, salt, pepper and nutmeg. Add the cheeses and mushroom mixture, and mix well. Pour into the tart shell and bake in the centre of the preheated oven for 45 minutes.

diva**dos**

 Add other wild mushrooms if you're feeling like a glamorous Diva!

 Make the pastry shell a day in advance, chill or freeze. Bake at least 6 hours before serving, and reheat to serve.

 Serve with Baby Green Salad, Fennel Slaw (see pages 135 and 134), or a warm potato salad with chive and walnut dressing.

diva**don'ts**

 Don't use cultivated white button mushrooms because they simply can't provide the intense flavour that a true Diva desires!

aubergine, goat's cheese and tomato galette with rocket and basil oil

● Serves: 8 ● Preparation: 45 minutes ● Cooking: 30 minutes

This tart looks like you've really gone to town, but most of the hard work has been done in advance. It makes a simple and stunning summer starter or light main course.

250 g/9 oz puff pastry

topping

100 ml (3½ fl oz) olive oil

1 onion, finely chopped

2 garlic cloves, chopped

1 tbsp thyme leaves

a good pinch of chopped rosemary leaves

2 medium aubergines, finely diced

125 g (4½ oz) soft goat's cheese

garnishes

15 g (½ oz) basil

75 ml (2½ fl oz) olive oil

salt and pepper

6 ripe plum tomatoes

1 tsp balsamic vinegar

125 g (4½ oz) rocket, washed

Parmesan shavings

1 Roll the pastry out on a lightly floured surface to 5 mm (¼ in) thick, and cut into 8 x 10 cm (4 in) circles using a cookie cutter. Chill for 30 minutes.

2 Meanwhile, preheat the oven to 200°C/400°F/Gas 6.

3 Line a baking tray with greaseproof paper and place the pastry circles on top. Prick several times with a fork and bake in the preheated oven for 7 minutes. Turn over, and bake for another 7 minutes until golden and crisp. Leave to cool.

4 For the topping, heat the olive oil in a large sauté pan, add the onion, garlic, thyme, and rosemary, and sauté until soft. Add the aubergine, and cook until everything is softened, about 15 minutes. Check the seasoning and allow to cool slightly before pureeing in a food processor

with the goat's cheese. Store, covered, in a cool place until needed.

5 To make the basil oil, place the basil, 4 tbsp of the olive oil, and some salt and pepper into a food processor and blend well. Store covered until needed.

6 Slice the tomatoes thinly and place in a bowl. Drizzle over the remaining olive oil, the balsamic vinegar, salt, and pepper, and leave to marinate for at least 30 minutes.

7 To assemble the galette, place each pastry circle on a serving plate and spread a spoonful of aubergine mixture on top. Arrange the tomato slices in a neat circle on top and garnish with a few rocket leaves and a large Parmesan shaving. Drizzle the basil oil around the edge of the plate. Serve at room temperature.

diva**dos**

 We use a mild goat's cheese, but you could use cream cheese.

 The galette can be assembled 1 hour before serving, but add the rocket, Parmesan and basil oil at the last minute.

 Serve the aubergine puree with our Diva Breadsticks (see page 158).

diva**don'ts**

 Don't use large beef tomatoes; they are too watery and less tasty than plum or vine-ripened tomatoes.

roasted tomato and shallot tarte tatin

● Serves: 8 ● Preparation: 1 hour ● Cooking: 30 minutes

Sweet roasted tomatoes and shallots are nestled in a balsamic syrup on a puff pastry crust. Great for summer parties as an elegant vegetarian dish.

250 g (9 oz) puff pastry

filling

20 medium Roma tomatoes, skinned (see page 22) and halved

125 ml (4 fl oz) olive oil

4 tbsp balsamic vinegar

2 garlic cloves, finely chopped

salt and pepper

12 small shallots, peeled

2 tbsp extra virgin olive oil

125 g (4½ oz) caster sugar

14 tbsp water

115 g (4 oz) Parmesan, freshly grated

1 Preheat the oven to 200°C/ 400°F/Gas 6. Place the tomato halves in a shallow roasting tin, pour over the olive oil and vinegar and sprinkle with garlic, salt, and pepper. Bake for 50 minutes and then slide off on to a large plate.

2 Roll out the puff pastry on a floured surface to fit a 28 cm (11 in) shallow tart or cake tin (or make 8 individual tarts). Place the rolled pastry on a plate and chill for 30 minutes. Line the tart tin with greaseproof paper. (If using a heavy cake tin or tarte tatin pan, the paper is not needed.)

3 Place the shallots in a small roasting tin, sprinkle with the extra virgin olive oil, and season with salt and pepper. Bake for 20 minutes, shaking several times to glaze.

4 Combine the sugar with the water in a saucepan and make a caramel as on page 40. Pour into the base of the prepared tin.

5 Firmly pack the tomato halves, cut side up, over the base of the prepared tin. Fill gaps with the shallots and sprinkle with Parmesan. Place the rolled pastry over the filling, and tuck the edges in to fit. Prick the pastry 6 times with a fork.

6 Bake in the oven at the same temperature for 30–40 minutes until the pastry is puffed and golden. Let the tart cool for 5 minutes before turning out. Run a knife around the edge of the tart, then invert on to a warm plate.

diva**dos**

Use plum or vine-ripened tomatoes in season; other types of tomato will be too watery.

Prepare the tart the day before. This enhances the flavours and makes it easier to turn out and then slice.

Serve with wild rocket and shaved fennel salad as a main dish.

If you double the recipe, then make 2 separate 28 cm (11 in) tarts. Roast the tomatoes in 2 separate pans.

diva**don'ts**

Don't reheat until 20 minutes before serving. Don't overcrowd the tomatoes, since this will create too much water during cooking. Divide between 2 pans if necessary. Don't leave the tomatoes in the hot tin, otherwise they will continue cooking.

smoked fish tart with crème fraîche, lemon and parmesan

● Serves: 8   ● Preparation: 1 hour   ● Cooking: 25 minutes

We love this creamy, delicate fish tart. Serve warm for lunch with a watercress, chicory, and avocado salad, and a mustard vinaigrette.

lemon and paprika pastry

85 g (3 oz) butter, chilled and diced

175 g (6 oz) plain flour

grated zest of 1 lemon

a pinch of pepper

½ tsp paprika

1 medium egg

filling

500 g (1 lb 2 oz) undyed smoked haddock, skinned and boned

2 bunches of spring onions, trimmed

25 g (1 oz) butter

2 medium eggs

2 medium egg yolks

225 ml (8 fl oz) crème fraîche

grated zest and juice of 1 lemon

85 g (3 oz) Parmesan, freshly grated

25 g (1 oz) dill or fennel herb, chopped

1 To make the pastry, place all the pastry ingredients except the egg in a food processor and blend until like breadcrumbs. Add the egg and pulse to a dough. If necessary, add a little cold water. Roll out on a lightly floured surface to line a deep 20 cm (8 in), loose-bottomed tart tin. Chill for 30 minutes.

2 Preheat the oven to 180°C/ 350°F/Gas 4.

3 Blind-bake the pastry case (see page 48) for 10 minutes. Remove the paper and beans and bake for another 5 minutes to crisp the bottom. Remove from the oven.

4 For the filling, cut the fish and spring onions into 2.5 cm (1 in) chunks. Melt the butter in a large frying pan, add the onions and sauté until slightly browned. Add the fish and cook for 2 minutes, then spoon this mixture into the tart shell.

5 Whisk together the eggs, egg yolks, crème fraîche, lemon zest and juice, Parmesan, and herb, and pour over the fish. Bake for 25 minutes, or until just set. Allow to stand for 30 minutes before serving.

diva**dos**

 Any smoked fish will work well for this recipe. Leeks can be used instead of spring onions, but need longer cooking.

 The pastry could be made and frozen, uncooked, 1 week before, or refrigerated the day before. The whole tart could be made the day before, then chilled and reheated to serve.

 Garnish with chives and wedges of lemon, and serve with a green salad and gutsy dressing (try our Classic Vinaigrette on page 118).

diva**don'ts**

 Don't cook the fish through in the pan – just brown it, since it will be cooked thoroughly in the oven.

pastry

Making pastry is a lot of fun and with adding extra flavourings, you can vary the classic shortcrust and sweet shortcrust to suit any tart filling. It can be made well ahead and freezes beautifully unbaked. Once the shell is baked, it should be filled and eaten within 24 hours.

CORE INGREDIENTS

Butter: We prefer the flavour of salted butter in sweet and savoury pastry. Ensure that the butter is chilled and cut into cubes for making pastry. On warm summer days, it helps to use frozen butter.

Italian OO Flour: This is the best flour for making pastry because of its fine texture. The Italians use it for making pasta but not bread, as it is too finely milled. When buying, look for an Italian flour with the double zero on the label. It's easily available now from larger supermarkets and speciality shops.

Wholemeal Flour: Wholemeal flour works well mixed with white flour to make a savoury, nutty-flavoured pastry.

Plain Flour: If Italian OO flour is unavailable, use finely milled plain white flour. Store all flours in their bags on a cool, dry and airy shelf. They will keep for 6 months.

Sugars: Different sugars can be used for making sweet pastries to vary the flavour and texture. Most often caster sugar is used, but do try golden caster sugar for a slightly honeyed flavour. Soft brown sugar and light muscovado sugar are also excellent, especially for warm winter fruit tarts.

Salt and Pepper: For savoury pastry, we like to add a pinch of sea salt and ground black pepper for extra flavour. Always use sea salt and freshly ground pepper, instead of pre-ground.

PUFF PASTRY

This rich, buttery pastry can be used for both sweet and savoury tarts. Home-made puff pastry is of course a dream, but we recommend good quality, ready-made puff pastry for convenience. Buy fresh or frozen and try to buy puff pastry made with butter rather than margarine. It can be frozen for 2 months or will keep for 1 week in the fridge. Always roll out thinly, pricking the base several times with a fork, and bake in a preheated hot oven.

FILO PASTRY

Again, buy good quality filo pastry, to use for both sweet and savoury recipes, and there's no need to make your own. Fresh filo pastry can be frozen but once it's defrosted, you cannot re-freeze. To use, remove the pastry from the packet and lay one sheet out on a lightly floured surface. Brush with melted butter, olive oil or beaten egg and use as directed in the recipe. Cover the pastry not in use with a damp tea-towel or clean cloth. We use filo to make canapé tartlets, which are extremely versatile. Keep stored in an airtight container for up to 1 month.

FLAVOUR ADDITIONS FOR SWEET PASTRY

Rosemary: Both fresh and dried rosemary are excellent in a sweetcrust – try using it for an orange or lemon tart. If using fresh, finely chop the spiky leaves in a food processor before adding to the pastry ingredients.

Cocoa Powder: It's worth buying a good quality dark cocoa powder, such as organic, for its rich and bitter flavour. We often add sifted cocoa powder to a sweet shortcrust pastry. For 225g (8oz) pastry, one tart shell, add 25g (1oz) cocoa to replace 25g (1oz) of the flour. Try Double Chocolate Mascarpone Tart (see page 150) or a summer berry tart with a dark chocolate pastry.

Orange and Lemon Zest: Ideal added to a sweet pastry, especially when using summer fruits. Add about 1 teaspoon grated zest to the pastry ingredients.

Almonds and Hazelnuts: Ground nuts in pastry add a delicious richness. However, they do make the pastry more oily to handle, so keep ingredients well chilled. Nuts can be roasted before using, at 180°C/350°F/Gas 4 for 10 minutes until golden. Cool then grind in a food processor. We recommend 25g (1oz) ground nuts to 200g (7oz) flour, 115g (4oz) chilled butter, 1 tablespoon caster sugar and 1 small egg. Always check the use-by date on nuts, as they stale quickly.

FLAVOUR ADDITIONS FOR SAVOURY PASTRY

Olives: Use rinsed and dried green or black pitted olives, and finely chop first by hand or in a food processor with the other pastry ingredients. Olives are very moist, so you'll need less egg or water to bind. Olive pastry has a lovely dark colour and a distinctive flavour.

Fresh Herbs: Finely chopped basil, parsley, thyme, rosemary, sage and oregano are all great additions to savoury pastry. Mix in by hand or, for better colour and flavour, mix with the other ingredients in a food processor.

Parmesan: Parmesan is a dry cheese, so when freshly grated and added to pastry ingredients, it works extremely well. Omit salt when using Parmesan, as it's already salty.

basic shortcrust pastry

● Preparation: 10 minutes   ● Cooking: 15 minutes

This recipe makes enough pastry to line a large 25cm (10in) tart case or 12 individual tins.

basic shortcrust pastry

250 g (9 oz) plain flour

salt and pepper

125 g (4½ oz) salted butter, chilled and diced

1 medium free-range egg

a dash of chilled water if needed

olive pastry

Add to the Basic Shortcrust Pastry 25 g (1 oz) chopped pitted olives or 1 tbsp olive puree with the egg.

parmesan pastry

Add to the Basic Shortcrust Pastry 25 g (1 oz) grated Parmesan with black pepper and or ¼ tsp cayenne pepper with the flour, first removing 25 g (1 oz) of the flour.

herb pastry

If adding drier herbs such as rosemary and thyme, use 1 tbsp.

175 g (6 oz) plain flour

85 g (3 oz) salted butter, chilled and diced

25 g (1 oz) flat-leaf or curly parsley (or basil or coriander), washed and dried

salt and pepper

1 medium free-range egg

basic shortcrust pastry

1 Place the flour, a pinch each of salt and pepper and the butter in a food processor. Process until the mixture resembles fine breadcrumbs. Add the egg and process until the pastry forms a ball. At this point you may add a dash of cold water if the egg is not binding the pastry together.

2 On a lightly floured surface, roll the pastry out thinly to line a loose-bottomed tart tin (or individual tins). Trim the tart by passing the rolling pin over the top edges. Place in the fridge for 30 minutes to rest, or freeze for 15 minutes.

3 Preheat the oven to 190°C/ 375°F/Gas 5.

4 To blind-bake the pastry case, line it with a large piece of foil or greaseproof paper. Fill with baking beans and spread them evenly over the base. (If you do not have baking beans available, use dried chickpeas or uncooked rice).

5 Bake the pastry case for 10 minutes, then remove the paper and beans, and bake for another 5 minutes to crisp the base. Remove from the oven, and set aside until needed.

herb pastry

1 Place the flour, butter, herbs, salt and pepper into a food processor and pulse until the parsley is well chopped and the flour has turned green.

2 Add the egg, and pulse until the ingredients form a dough. Chill and use as required in the recipe.

filo tarts of smoked salmon, tomato, and dill with cucumber-lime salsa

● Serves: 8 ● Preparation: 45 minutes ● Cooking: 20 minutes

Smoked salmon never seems to waver in popularity. Here it's paired with crisp filo and wrapped around crème fraîche, served with a crunchy cucumber salsa.

16 large filo pastry sheets

55 g (2 oz) butter, melted

500 g (1 lb 2 oz) ripe tomatoes, seeded, skinned and chopped

2 tsp oregano, chopped

salt and pepper

6 tsp crème fraîche

350 g (12 oz) smoked salmon

cucumber-lime salsa

½ cucumber

15 g (½ oz) dill

3 spring onions, finely chopped

juice of 1 lime

1 tbsp olive oil

1 For the salsa, cut the cucumber in half. Seed by running a teaspoon down the centre. Finely chop the cucumber flesh and mix with all the remaining salsa ingredients. Season to taste, cover and chill until needed.

2 Preheat the oven to 160°C/ 325°F/Gas 3.

3 Brush each filo sheet with melted butter and fold each in half. Place 2 filo sheets on top of each other at differing angles, and wedge into 8 x 10 cm (4 in) shallow, loose-bottomed tart tins. Chill for 30 minutes.

4 Mix the chopped tomatoes with the oregano, salt, and pepper, and divide between the 8 tarts. Bake in the oven for 8 minutes, until the pastry is crisp and lightly browned.

5 Remove from the oven, spoon the crème fraîche on top of the tomatoes, arrange the smoked salmon around and return to the oven for 2 minutes.

6 Pop the tarts out of the tins, and place on serving plates. Spoon a tbsp of the salsa on top of each, or to one side.

divados

 Smoked trout can be used instead of salmon; soured cream could replace the crème fraîche; and tarragon could replace the oregano. All filo sheets vary in size, so 16 sheets is an approximate guide only.

 The filo cases can be kept, unbaked, in the fridge overnight. The salsa can be made up to 6 hours before, but do not add the lime juice, olive oil, salt and pepper until 30 minutes beforehand.

 Serve as an elegant starter before Grilled Swordfish or Chilli-crusted Beef Fillet (see pages 97 and 60).

divadon'ts

 Don't allow the edges of the filo tarts to burn.

winter squash, roasted garlic, and gorgonzola galette

● Serves: 8 ● Preparation: 1 hour ● Cooking: 30 minutes

An excellent vegetarian dish for a cold winter night. Butternut squash gets a touch of glamour from this irresistible combination of roasted garlic, sage and creamy Gorgonzola!

250 g (9 oz) puff pastry

1 egg, beaten

filling

1 kg (2 lb 4 oz) butternut squash

olive oil

salt and pepper

1 garlic bulb

1 small onion, finely chopped

10 fresh sage leaves, coarsely chopped

125 g (4½ oz) Parmesan, freshly grated

100 g (3½ oz) Gorgonzola, in chunks

1 Preheat the oven to 200°C/ 400°F/Gas 6. Using a large sharp knife, halve the squash. Scrape out and discard the seeds and fibres using a spoon. Lightly brush each cut side of the squash with olive oil, and season with salt and pepper. Place the squash cut side down on a baking sheet. Tear the garlic bulb apart, but do not peel. Place the cloves under the squash, and drizzle everything with olive oil. Bake for about 1 hour, or until the squash is tender when pierced. Scoop the flesh out into a large bowl. Squeeze the garlic out of its skin and add to the squash.

2 Meanwhile, on a lightly floured surface, roll out the puff pastry into a 33 cm (13 in) round. Prick the base 6 times with a fork, place the pastry on a flat plate and chill for 30 minutes.

3 To finish the filling, warm 2 tsp olive oil in a small saucepan over a low heat. Add the onion and sage, and cook until soft. Add to the squash along with the Parmesan. Mash with a wooden spoon or potato masher to combine well. Season with salt and pepper and fold in the Gorgonzola.

4 Preheat the oven to the same temperature. Place a large, flat, slightly oiled baking sheet in to heat. Place the squash filling into the centre of the pastry circle, spreading evenly and leaving a 5 cm (2 in) border. Fold the border over the filling, which will leave the centre of the filling showing. Brush the overlapping pastry with the beaten egg.

5 To bake the galette, slide it off the plate on to the preheated baking tray. Bake until the crust is nicely browned, about 25 minutes. Serve hot or warm.

diva**dos**

 You could use other blue cheeses, like Roquefort.

 Make the tart filling the day before. Roll out the tart shell the day before. Fill to bake. This galette reheats well.

 Make individual galette tarts for a small gathering – they look very elegant. Serve with a simple green salad with a Classic Vinaigrette (see page 118).

filo tart with charmoula chicken

- Serves: 8 • Preparation: 2 hours marinating plus 1 hour • Cooking: 30 minutes

Charmoula is a garlicky marinade from North Africa that's used to flavour just about every kind of food there. We've marinated chicken in it, before wrapping it up in crisp filo pastry and serving it with a spicy tomato jam.

approx. 10 –16 filo pastry sheets

6 tbsp melted butter

chicken filling

750 g (1 lb 10 oz) boneless, skinless chicken breasts, diced

1 red onion, finely chopped

1 large carrot, finely diced

salt and pepper

1 tbsp olive oil

100 g (3½ oz) pine kernels, toasted

2 eggs, beaten

charmoula marinade

1 large bunch of fresh coriander, finely chopped

1 large bunch of flat-leaf parsley, finely chopped

6 garlic cloves, crushed

1 tbsp each of ground cumin, ground coriander and paprika

1 tsp each of saffron strands and cayenne pepper

juice of 2 lemons

4 tbsp extra virgin olive oil

1 tsp sea salt

to serve

2 x Moroccan Tomato Jam recipe (see page 27)

1 Mix the marinade ingredients together and pour over the diced chicken. Leave for at least 2 hours (or ideally marinate overnight) in a cool place.

2 Sauté the onion and carrot in the oil until soft. Add the chicken, salt and pepper, and pan-fry for 5 minutes until opaque. Then drain the chicken in a large colander in order to get rid of any liquid that might make the pastry soggy. In a large bowl, combine the chicken, pine kernels, egg, salt and pepper.

3 You can make several individual parcels or 1 large filo tart. To serve individual parcels, lay 2 pieces of buttered filo pastry on top of each other. Spoon approximately 100 g (3½ oz) of the filling on the top of the filo, and then start to roll it up like a large spring roll, tucking the edges in as you roll. Brush with butter. Repeat the process to make 8 parcels. They should then be chilled until ready to bake.

4 To make 1 large tart, brush 6 filo sheets with butter and lay over the base of a loose-bottomed 20 cm (8 in) tart tin at different angles so that you cover the whole base, leaving the extra pastry hanging over the side. Place the chicken filling inside, bringing the pastry back over it at jagged angles. Brush 4 more filo sheets with butter, and crunch up on top of the pie. Chill till ready to bake.

5 Preheat the oven to 160°C/ 325°F/Gas 3. Place a flat baking tray or trays into the oven to become hot.

6 Place the pie(s) on the hot tray(s) and bake for 30 minutes. Turn the individual parcels once, then remove from the oven. If baking a large pie, take the pie out of the tart tin using oven gloves, and place back on the baking sheet to crisp the bottom. Bake for a further 10 minutes.

7 If serving hot, eat immediately with the tomato jam, or eat at room temperature, but do not reheat again.

diva**dos**

  Assemble the pie(s) in the morning and chill.

  Excellent served with any other tomato relish or chutney.

diva**don'ts**

  Don't use the very thin, papery Greek filo pastry, as it is not easy to work with.

broccoli, italian sausage and pecorino tart with roasted cherry tomatoes

- Serves: 8   - Preparation: 45 minutes   - Cooking: 25 minutes

Broccoli di rapa (or purple-sprouting broccoli) is a new Italian vegetable. Once blanched and pan-fried in garlic, it is deliciously crunchy and full of flavour. We've combined it with Italian sausage, Pecorino and oven-dried tomatoes for a tart you won't forget.

350 g (12 oz) all-butter puff pastry

salt and pepper

topping

400 g (14 oz) broccoli di rapa, or other sprouting green (16 stalks)

1 garlic clove, finely chopped

5 tbsp olive oil

500 g (1 lb 2 oz) Italian pork sausage, skins removed

1 tsp fennel seeds

1 tsp dried red chilli, crushed

85 g (3 oz) Pecorino cheese, grated

roasted cherry tomatoes

24 ripe cherry tomatoes, halved

2 tbsp olive oil

1 tbsp balsamic vinegar

garnishes

1 large ball of fresh mozzarella, ripped into pieces

25 g (1 oz) basil, torn

1 Roll out the pastry, and cut into a 30 cm (12 in) circle. Alternatively, you can make 4 individual tarts that should be rolled out to 15 cm (6 in) circles. Place on greaseproof paper and chill for 30 minutes.

2 Preheat the oven to 200°C/ 400°F/Gas 6. Place the cherry tomato halves on a baking tray, and sprinkle with oil, vinegar, salt and pepper. Bake for 20 minutes and remove. Increase the oven to 220°C/425°F/Gas 7, and heat 1 or 2 large baking sheets for 15 minutes.

3 Cut the broccoli into 2.5 cm (1 in) pieces and blanch for 2 minutes in salted boiling water. Plunge into cold water, then drain and dry on a tea-towel. Sauté the garlic in 3 tbsp of the oil, add the broccoli and cook for a minute, stirring. Season with salt and pepper.

4 Heat the remaining oil in a sauté pan. Add the sausage, fennel seeds, chilli, salt and pepper. Pan-fry, using a flat spoon to break the sausage into chunks, until browned.

5 Arrange the broccoli over the pastry circles, leaving a 2.5 cm (1 in) border. Divide the sausage, Pecorino and tomatoes between the tart(s). Fold the pastry border over the filling, pleating it as you go around.

6 Remove the baking sheet(s) from the oven and slide the tart(s) on to it or them. The heat will help the bottom pastry to crisp. Bake for 10 minutes, then lower the oven temperature to 200°C/400°F/Gas 6 and cook for another 15 minutes or until the pastry is golden.

7 Remove the tart(s) from the oven and immediately scatter over the mozzarella and basil. Serve warm.

divados

 Buy the best-quality Italian spicy-garlicky or herbed sausages.

 The tart can be prepared in the morning and reheated in a hot oven for 10 minutes to serve.

divadon'ts

 Don't forget to put the broccoli into cold water after blanching, otherwise it will lose its brilliant green colour.

diva**meats**

teriyaki beef fillet with noodles and soy dipping sauce

• Serves: 8   • Preparation: overnight marinating and 45 minutes   • Cooking: 15 minutes

Here's one of our favourites for Japanese style, purity and taste.

1 x 1 kg (2 lb 4 oz) beef fillet

4 tbsp cracked black peppercorns

500 g (1 lb 2 oz) Japanese green tea or soba noodles

4 tbsp toasted sesame oil

2 tbsp sesame seeds, toasted

24 fresh asparagus spears, trimmed

1 tbsp light soy sauce

salt and pepper

marinade

250 ml (9 fl oz) light soy sauce

150 ml (5 fl oz) saké

4 tbsp caster sugar

10 garlic cloves, crushed

10 spring onions, chopped

1 tsp crushed red chilli

2 tsp toasted sesame oil

soy dipping sauce

125 ml (4 fl oz) light soy sauce

75 ml (2½ fl oz) rice wine vinegar

2 tbsp water

1 tbsp crushed garlic

3 tsp caster sugar

1 tsp hot chilli bean paste

2 spring onions, thinly sliced

1 Mix all the marinade ingredients together and place in a plastic bag or snug container with the beef fillet for at least 2 hours or overnight.

2 Preheat the oven to 200°C/ 400°F/Gas 6. Wipe excess marinade from the meat, and press cracked peppercorns all over. Sear the fillet in a hot pan, on all sides.

3 Cook the noodles in salted boiling water until al dente. Drain well and toss with half the sesame oil and sesame seeds.

4 Char-grill or sauté the asparagus until tender and then toss with the remaining sesame oil, the soy sauce, salt and pepper.

5 Finish cooking the meat by roasting in the preheated oven for 15 minutes or until cooked to your liking – medium rare for us. Let it rest for 5 minutes before thinly slicing.

6 Place the sliced beef, garnished with asparagus, on a large platter. Swirl noodles decoratively next to it. Prepare guests individual small bowls of the dipping sauce alongside their plates, with chopsticks to serve themselves.

diva**dos**

Order an evenly shaped beef fillet from your butcher. We advise asking him to tie the meat, as this helps it to cook evenly and helps with presentation.

The meat can be served hot or cold. If serving cold, you can roast in the morning, keep in a cool place and slice just before serving. Cook the noodles the day before, drain, place in a bowl of cold water, cover and keep in the fridge. When ready to serve, drain well and dress with oil and seeds. Both the sauces can be made ahead of time, making this the perfect summer party dish!

For warm serving, sear the meat in the morning and finish off the roasting in a preheated oven just before serving.

lamb fillet with roasted garlic, coriander and yogurt sauce

● Serves: 8   ● Preparation: overnight marinating and 20 minutes   ● Cooking: 1 hour

This is a divine sauce for lamb or beef fillet. Roast garlic, coriander, and balsamic vinegar are swirled into creamy Greek yogurt. The result is outrageous!

1 kg (2 lb 4 oz) lamb fillet
(eye of the loin)

2 tsp cumin seeds, crushed

olive oil

4 garlic cloves, crushed

salt and pepper

200 g (7 oz) young spinach leaves

a handful of fresh herbs
(parsley, thyme, oregano)

100 g (3½ oz) pine kernels, toasted

sauce

2 garlic bulbs

1 tbsp olive oil

150 ml (5 fl oz) Greek yogurt

1 tsp Dijon mustard

2 tbsp balsamic vinegar

½ tsp cumin seeds, toasted

1 tsp coriander seeds, toasted

freshly grated nutmeg

1 Rub the lamb all over with the cumin, 2 tbsp oil and garlic, cover well and leave to marinate for several hours or overnight in the fridge.

2 For the sauce, preheat the oven to 180°C/350°F/Gas 4. Slice off the top quarter of the garlic bulbs to expose the cloves. Put the bulbs on pieces of foil, sprinkle with olive oil, salt and pepper, wrap up and bake for 45 minutes. Cool slightly before squeezing the garlic pulp from the skins. Puree the pulp with the rest of the sauce ingredients and some salt and pepper in a food processor. Taste for seasoning.

3 Preheat the oven to 220°C/425°F/Gas 7. Season the lamb fillet, and sear to brown on all sides in 2 tbsp oil in a hot frying pan. Roast in the preheated oven for 15 minutes, or until cooked but still pink. Remove from the oven and rest for 5 minutes in a warm place.

4 To serve, pile the spinach and herbs on a large platter. Slice the lamb, arrange it over the spinach, spoon the sauce next to the lamb and scatter with the pine kernels.

divados

 Use large fresh garlic bulbs that don't have green sprouts.

 Sear the meat in the morning and roast just before serving. Prepare the sauce in the morning and chill. Bring back to room temperature before serving.

 Serve with potato cakes or Saffron-roasted Potatoes (see page 138).

divadon'ts

 Don't use old spices – be sure they are fresh by their strong fragrance.

 Don't heat the sauce or it will separate. Always serve it at room temperature.

slow-roasted tuscan pork with fennel

● Serves: 8 ● Preparation: 10 minutes ● Cooking: about 4–5 hours

There is nothing like lusty hunks of pork that fall to pieces when you cut the strings off. What's the secret? Inexpensive meat! Only leg and shoulder cuts, with their marbles of fat, can produce this result.

2.25 kg/5 lb boneless pork shoulder or leg, tied (crackling removed)

4 garlic cloves, cut into slivers

3 tbsp olive oil

1 tbsp each of salt and pepper

2 tbsp dried oregano

2 tbsp finely chopped rosemary

15 g (½ oz) fennel seeds

2 tsp dried chilli flakes

125 ml (4 fl oz) dry white wine

55 g (2 oz) butter, chilled and finely diced

to serve

lots of fresh herbs

1 Preheat the oven to 140°C/275°F/Gas 1.

2 Take a sharp knife and cut small slits into the meat. Insert the slivers of garlic all over the meat. Rub with 1 tbsp of the olive oil and the salt and pepper. In a very large frying pan, sear the meat on all sides until browned.

3 Rub the remaining oil over the pork and then roll in a mixture of the herbs and spices. Arrange on a rack in a roasting tin. Place in the preheated low oven and cook for about 4–5 hours. The meat will be tender and fall apart when the string is removed.

4 Slice the pork and place on a platter with rosemary sprigs and other fresh herbs.

5 Spoon off any excess fat from the roasting juices and bring the juices to the boil. Add the wine, simmer for 5 minutes and, when ready to serve, whisk in the butter. Serve hot poured over the pork.

diva**dos**

 Try and get a roast that is no more than 13 cm/5 in in diameter so that it's long and thin.

 Make the spice rub ahead, and store in a jar.

 Serve with Celeriac and Roasted Garlic Puree, Saffron-roasted Potatoes or Gratin of Balsamic Wild Mushrooms (see pages 131, 136 and 109). Use any leftover meat to make a delectable salad or sandwiches the next day.

diva**don'ts**

 Don't use pork loin – it will be too lean to cook for a long time.

 Don't be tempted to cook at a higher temperature – it's the slow cooking that makes the meat so wonderfully tender.

pomegranate-marinated lamb cutlets with coriander tabbouleh

● Serves: 8 ● Preparation: overnight marinating and 1 hour ● Cooking: 15 minutes

Please don't run when you see this long list of ingredients – it's not as bad as you think! The lovely tart pomegranate dressing is wonderful on the lamb.

3 tbsp pomegranate molasses

1 tbsp olive oil

2 garlic cloves, chopped

grated zest of 1 lemon

salt and pepper

24 lamb cutlets, trimmed

pomegranate dressing

90 ml (3 fl oz) olive oil

4 tbsp pomegranate molasses

juice of ½ lemon

1 garlic clove

1 tbsp clear honey

15 g (1 oz) mint

coriander tabbouleh

300 g (10½ oz) cracked bulgar wheat

1 tsp coriander seeds, toasted and ground

½ tsp each of cumin and fennel seeds, toasted and ground

1 red onion, finely chopped

1 tsp salt

½ cucumber, seeded

4 tomatoes, seeded

25 g (1 oz) each of parsley and coriander, finely chopped

15 g (½ oz) mint, finely chopped

4 spring onions, finely chopped

juice and grated zest of 1 lemon

cayenne pepper

4 tbsp olive oil

1 Mix together the pomegranate molasses, olive oil, garlic, lemon zest, salt and pepper, rub into the lamb, and leave for 2 hours or overnight.

2 For the pomegranate dressing, place all the ingredients into a food processor and puree. Taste to check the seasoning.

3 To make the tabbouleh, wash the bulgar wheat in several changes of water and drain. Place the wheat in a large bowl, cover with 2.5 cm (1 in) cold water, and soak for an hour. Drain the wheat, pressing down

hard to extract as much water as possible. Mix with the remaining ingredients and toss well. Taste and adjust the seasoning if necessary.

4 Grill the cutlets under a hot grill or on a barbecue, brushing with the marinade and turning to make sure both sides are cooked and glazed properly.

5 Serve on a large platter with the tabbouleh piled high in the centre, the lamb cutlets around the edge and the pomegranate dressing drizzled over the lamb.

diva**dos**

 Lamb steaks can be used instead of cutlets. If pomegranate molasses is not available, you can use lemon rind and juice, mixed with clear honey. It is now sold in some supermarkets, so buy a few bottles and have on hand. It's a great unusual flavouring to have in the kitchen. Use couscous instead of bulgar wheat. Prepare according to packet directions.

 Marinate the lamb and make the dressing the day before. Prepare all the ingredients for the tabbouleh the day before, but mix together with olive oil and lemon juice 2 hours before serving.

 Start with the Salad Mezze Plate, or serve with Moroccan Carrots (see pages 122 and 133).

chilli-crusted beef fillet with ancho and field mushroom sauce

● Serves: 8　● Preparation: 45 minutes　● Cooking: 20 minutes

A traditional red wine mushroom sauce for beef fillet is boosted by an extra kick of flavour from ancho chillies. These mild dried Mexican chillies are available at most supermarkets and have a smoky, fruity taste. Great with fried polenta or potato mash on a cold winter evening.

2 tbsp mild Mexican chilli powder

1 tbsp cumin seeds, toasted and ground

1 tbsp extra virgin olive oil

1 kg (2 lb 4 oz) beef fillet, trimmed of excess fat.

4 tbsp finely chopped flat-leaf parsley

sauce

4 large red dried ancho chillies

4 tbsp olive oil

1 medium onion, finely chopped

4 large garlic cloves, crushed

500 ml (18 fl oz) dry red wine

500 g (18 oz) field mushrooms, chopped

250 ml (9 fl oz) chicken stock

4 tbsp clear honey

1 Combine the chilli powder, ground cumin and oil. Rub all over the meat and leave covered for several hours. The fillet can be cut into 8 thick steaks, or roasted whole and carved to serve.

2 To start the sauce, stem and seed the dried chillies. Lightly toast for 30 seconds in a hot, dry saucepan. Soak in boiling water for 15 minutes, before pureeing in a food processor. Push through a sieve and set aside. You should have about 125 ml (4 fl oz).

3 Heat the olive oil in a large saucepan, add the onion and garlic and cook over low heat until soft.

Increase the heat, stir in the red wine and boil until reduced by half. Add the mushrooms, stock, chilli and honey, and simmer for about 15 minutes.

4 Preheat a heavy griddle, frying pan or char-grill, or preheat the oven to 200°C/400°F/Gas 6. If serving steaks, sear the meat until done to your liking; if serving a whole fillet, sear on all sides, then complete the cooking in the preheated oven for 20 minutes.

5 Allow the whole fillet to rest before carving. Serve slices or steaks on a bed of mushroom sauce, sprinkled with the parsley.

divados

 Make the sauce the day before, and reheat before serving.

 Serve with Saffron-roasted Potatoes or Asian Potato Cakes (see pages 138 and 104).

 Reduce the sauce so that it is not watery. Keep it boiling until it turns glossy and thick.

divadon'ts

 Don't purchase dry and brittle ancho chillies. They should be supple like a piece of soft leather. Refrigerated, they will keep for at least 6 months.

mojo-marinated steaks with coriander sauce and chilean salsa

● Serves: 8   ● Preparation: overnight marinating and 15 minutes   ● Cooking: 20 minutes

This could be the easiest dinner you have ever prepared – if you have a food processor! Mojo is a zesty, cumin-spiked marinade that's used by many cultures in South America.

1 kg (2 lb 4 oz) boned beef sirloin or fillet in one piece

mojo marinade

5 garlic cloves, finely chopped

1 tsp each of salt and pepper

juice of 2 oranges

2 tsp ground cumin

125 ml (4 fl oz) extra virgin olive oil

coriander sauce

55 g (2 oz) fresh coriander

1 green chilli, finely chopped

1 small red onion, finely diced

2 tbsp red wine vinegar (Cabernet Sauvignon)

125 ml (4 fl oz) extra virgin olive oil

1 tsp each of salt and pepper

chilean salsa

1 medium red onion, chopped

a small handful of fresh coriander

250 g (9 oz) cherry tomatoes (pomodorino if available)

1½ tsp mild sweet paprika (Spanish pimentón)

½ tsp cayenne pepper

1 tsp salt

125 ml (4 fl oz) extra virgin olive oil

90 ml (3 fl oz) red wine vinegar (Cabernet Sauvignon)

1 Combine the marinade ingredients, pour over the beef, cover and chill overnight. Turn several times during marinating.

2 For the sauce, pulse the coriander and chilli in a food processor until roughly chopped. Place in a small bowl and add the onion, vinegar, olive oil, salt and pepper.

3 Pulse all the Chilean salsa ingredients except the oil and vinegar in the food processor until a chunky puree. Add the vinegar and oil, pulse again and then scrape into a bowl.

4 There are two ways to cook the beef: you can barbecue, or you can sear the beef in a hot frying pan to brown on all sides, then roast for 20 minutes in a preheated oven at 200°C/400°F/Gas 6. Remove the beef, cover loosely in foil and rest for 10 minutes.

5 Thinly slice the beef and place on a large platter with bowls of Chilean salsa and coriander sauce next to it for guests to help themselves.

diva**dos**

 Try to use pimentón, the smoky Spanish paprika, as the flavour is amazing.

 The coriander sauce can be made the day before, covered and chilled. Bring back to room temperature to serve. Make the Chilean salsa several hours before serving.

 The beef can be served hot or cold. Serve after Spiced Chicken Empanaditas (see page 30), and accompany with crisp potato wedges, roasted in a very hot oven with olive oil, salt and pepper, and Tamarind-roasted Vegetables (see page 128).

diva**don'ts**

 Don't slice the meat until just before serving.

meats

For those of us who love it, there is nothing like the wafting aroma of a good joint of meat being seared with black pepper or a pork roast crackling away in the oven. If your wallet can withstand it, free range and organic are best for quality and taste. Regardless of what grade or cut is purchased, we are huge advocates of marinades, which uplift the flavour of any meat. Most of our recipes use fillets, sliced steaks and cutlets, which are not only elegant but simple for guests to eat at a party. We feel it is far better to purchase meat from a local butcher rather than supermarkets. This gives you the opportunity to communicate with your butcher personally about what you need, and will also enable you to learn more about different cuts, meats in season, quality, prices and, often, traditional cooking methods.

BEEF

Beef Fillet: The 'crème de la crème' of beef. It's so tender it doesn't require a knife, which is why it's perfect for *Diva Cooking*. We also like it because you can sear it off in the morning and finish cooking in a hot oven before the meal. Beef fillet lends itself to any piquant flavours: olives, anchovies, and garlic are just a few. It is wonderful marinated in red wine, soy sauce or fresh herbs. Look for pieces that are evenly shaped so that the meat will cook to the same degree of rareness all the way through. Or ask your butcher to string up the fillet; this will keep the meat evenly shaped while cooking, which is good for presentation! Try slicing the fillet 1 inch thick, marinade in garlic, paprika, black pepper and light soy sauce overnight. To serve, sear the steaks briefly on both sides on a hot griddle or barbecue, or simply in a hot, heavy-based frying pan. Try serving with Avocado-Lime Salsa (see page 17) as a light, fantastic Diva main course, or between two slices of fresh bread, with caramelised onion marmalade, crisp lettuce, Classic Mayonnaise (see page 118) and mustard to enjoy the best-ever steak sandwich!

Sirloin Steak: Like fillet, this is also an indulgent choice of meat. Sirloin is excellent for grilling and thinly slicing. Perfect for Thai Beef Salad, a Chilean-inspired steak or a teriyaki dish (see pages 126, 61 and 54), it works in any cuisine. Whilst it is enlightened with a sharp marinade, it is equally good grilled with just salt and pepper.

Skirt Steak: The poor stepsister to sirloin, this is not only economical but full of flavour. It is a long, flat piece of meat taken from the diaphragm muscle. Marinating is advised for skirt steak, which helps to tenderise it. Any strong flavours

such as garlic, soy sauce, red wine vinegar or herbs are perfect to do the job. Once seared and sliced thinly across the grain, it is similar to more expensive grades. Lovely grilled on the barbecue or stuffed, rolled and roasted. It is not found regularly at the butcher's, but they can easily cut it for you.

LAMB

Lamb Fillet: Also known as the 'eye of the loin', this extravagant cut is a special treat for lamb lovers. Used in similar dishes to beef fillet, it can adapt to any cuisine. Marinades only make it more delicious after absorbing flavours overnight. We find lamb fillet is excellent when catering for larger numbers. As there is little fat, once marinated it can be seared several hours before, placed on roasting trays and kept in a cool place until ready to be roasted in a hot oven. Carving is simple with no bones to tackle. The meat is extremely tender, and therefore suits barbecues well, or can be simply grilled for smaller parties. Such a versatile meat goes just as well with the classic sauces as it does pestos, salsas and the Middle Eastern flavours created by roasted spices, yogurts, citrus fruits and vegetables.

Leg of Lamb: For parties it's best to have your butcher butterfly the leg. Marinate it in something zingy such as soy sauce and copious amounts of

garlic, red wine and mint. Fresh herbs such as rosemary, thyme or oregano create a wonderful perfume when added before cooking. Excellent for serving large groups of people, it can be served with piquant sauces such as salsa verde, tomato and olive confit or mint dressing. It also works well roasted over potato gratins, or tightly covered and slowly roasted for up to 4 hours.

Lamb Cutlets: Cutlets are preferred to lamb chops as they are specifically taken from the ribcage. Chops from the neck or leg could be tougher and are not so desirable. These gorgeous little cutlets are easy to grill, love marinades and look very elegant. They work well with Mediterranean, Middle Eastern or Indian flavours. Ask your butcher to French-trim them, which means trimming all the fat off the long slender bones.

PORK

Pork Roasts: We like boneless pork roasts for parties as they're easy to prepare and look more refined than cutting the meat off the bone. Ask your butcher to bone and tie the meat for you. If you are roasting it, be sure to get the crackling fat, as you can always crisp it separately. The fat should be removed if you are braising. There are three types of roast, which are…

Loin: The most expensive cut, it requires a higher cooking temperature and shorter roasting time. It produces firm even slices for a smart presentation.

Shoulder: Although this is an inexpensive and tougher grade of meat, it can be sublime – try slow-roasting it on a low temperature in to create a sumptuous piece of meat. When you cut the strings off before serving, the meat falls into juicy tender pieces.

Leg: Exactly the same principles apply to the leg roast as the shoulder. It offers terrific value for money and an impressive result.

All pork roasts work fabulously with vinegar, garlic, herb and olive oil marinades. Try some balsamic vinegar, rosemary or thyme and olive oil to marinate the meat before roasting. Dry spices and herbs such as fennel seeds, oregano and chilli powder are excellent when rubbed over the roast while cooking. Always make sure that the roast is not sitting directly in the pan by propping it up with a rack. It's imperative that pork should always be cooked until it is no longer pink. Use a meat thermometer to gauge the internal temperature of 80°C/176°F, to make sure you don't overcook or dry the meat out.

butterflied leg of lamb with slow-roasted tomato, basil and olive confit

- Serves: 8   - Preparation: overnight marinating and 45 minutes
- Cooking: 3½ hours and 35 minutes

Soy sauce, wine, garlic and mint are the most exquisite marinade ingredients for any red meat. After slow-roasting or grilling, it becomes even more delicious with tomato confit. This is a great plan-ahead dish for large groups.

1 x 1.8kg (4 lb) leg of lamb, butterflied

marinade

175 ml (6 fl oz) red wine

90 ml (3 fl oz) light soy sauce

3 garlic cloves, chopped or crushed

15 g (½ oz) mint, chopped, plus extra for garnishing

confit

12 plum tomatoes, halved

2 garlic cloves, thinly sliced

200 ml (7 fl oz) olive oil

55 g (2 oz) black olives, pitted and chopped

12 basil leaves, torn, plus extra for garnishing

salt and pepper

1 Preheat the oven to 110°C/225°F/Gas ¼. To make the confit, place the tomato halves on a roasting tray with a slice of garlic on each. Drizzle with some of the olive oil, season with salt and pepper and roast for 3½ hours. Remove from the oven, cool and cut the tomatoes into large dice. Mix the tomatoes with the olives and basil, and stir in the remaining oil. Set aside.

2 To prepare the meat, remove any hunks of unwanted fat using a sharp knife, but leave some on for flavour. To flatten it, lay the meat on a work surface, fat side down. Make long cuts into the meat, one in the centre and one on each of the outside flaps. Place a piece of greaseproof paper over the meat and pound with a rolling pin until evenly flat. Place in a large bowl.

3 Mix the marinade ingredients together and pour over the meat. Marinate for 4 hours or overnight.

4 Preheat a barbecue, char-grill or grill. When hot, remove the lamb from the marinade and pat dry with kitchen paper. Cook for 40 minutes, or until pink, turning several times. Allow to rest for 10 minutes before carving.

5 Carve the meat on to a warm platter, serve with the confit and garnish with lots of extra herbs.

diva**dos**

 Ask your butcher to butterfly the lamb for you.

 The marinade can be made days before, covered and chilled, as can the confit (store in a screw-top jar and keep cool).

 The lamb is best marinated 24 hours ahead. Turn over several times during marinating.

 Excellent in the summer, or try in winter with Saffron or Red Pepper Aïoli (see pages 73 and 85). Serve with Fennel Slaw, Saffron-roasted Potatoes or Baby Green Salad (see pages 134, 138 and 135).

diva**don'ts**

 Don't use dark soy sauce as it is too salty.

gingered beef with honey and prunes

● Serves: 8   ● Preparation: 30 minutes   ● Cooking: 2 hours

Despite their dowdy reputation, prunes are a brilliant ingredient to cook with. Adding a subtle sweetness, they are ideal for spicy Moroccan tagines and stews.

1 kg (2 lb 4 oz) chuck or braising steak, sliced

plain flour

salt and pepper

olive oil

3 onions, finely chopped

2 garlic cloves, chopped

10 cm (4 in) piece of fresh root ginger, grated

3 tsp ground cumin

300 ml (10 fl oz) each of red wine and meat stock

2 tbsp clear honey

350 g (12 oz) ready-to-eat stoned prunes

1 tbsp pomegranate molasses

relish

1 red onion, finely sliced

15 g (½ oz) flat-leaf parsley, chopped

seeds of 1 pomegranate (optional)

1 tbsp olive oil

½ tbsp red wine vinegar

1 Cut the beef slices into 7.5 cm (3 in) pieces, and shake in flour, salt and pepper. Heat 2 tbsp olive oil in a large casserole, and sear the meat on both sides. Remove the meat and add a little more oil. Fry the onions, garlic and ginger for 10 minutes on a medium to high heat, then add the cumin and cook for another 2 minutes.

2 Return the meat to the pan, add the red wine, stock and honey, and bring to the boil. Add the prunes, cover and simmer for 1½ hours.

3 When checking the meat, you want it to be tender and easy to cut. Add the pomegranate molasses and cook for another 30 minutes. Cool a little with the lid on.

4 To make the relish, mix all the ingredients together and season to taste.

5 Serve the beef in a warm dish, garnished with the relish spooned on top.

diva**dos**

Make this casserole 1 or 2 days ahead, as the texture, colour and flavour will benefit enormously. If you are short on time, garnish with lots of parsley or coriander instead of the relish.

Make sure you simmer the meat over a very low heat, and keep it covered during cooking.

Start with the Spicy Prawns or Salad Mezze Plate (see pages 27 and 122), and serve with Celeriac and Roasted Garlic Puree (see page 131).

diva**don'ts**

Don't allow your butcher to dice the chuck steak as normal – make sure you buy sliced steak. Don't despair if you can't find pomegranates – the relish does work without.

roast fillet of beef with coriander and peanut pesto

● Serves: 8   ● Preparation: 4 hours marinating and 20 minutes   ● Cooking: 25 minutes

This superbly elegant dish is ideal for a summer fusion menu. It has serious flavour as well!

1 kg (2 lb 4 oz) beef fillet in one piece

1 tbsp olive oil

marinade

2 red chillies, seeded

2 garlic cloves, peeled

1 tbsp clear honey

4 tbsp olive oil

2 tbsp each of dark and light soy sauce

juice of 2 limes

coriander and peanut pesto

125 g (4½ oz) unsalted peanuts

1 bunch of spring onions, washed and dried

250 g (9 oz) fresh coriander

2 green chillies, seeded

2.5 cm (1 in) piece fresh root ginger, chopped

1 garlic clove, chopped

1 tbsp rice wine vinegar

juice of ½ lemon

1 tbsp teriyaki sauce

2 tbsp sesame oil

salt and pepper

1 To make the pesto, puree all the ingredients in a food processor. Taste to check the seasoning. Cover and chill until needed.

2 Trim the fillet of any excess fat with a sharp knife. Puree all the marinade ingredients in a food processor, then pour over the fillet. Leave the beef to marinate for 4 hours.

3 Preheat the oven to 200°C/ 400°F/Gas 6.

4 Remove the beef from the marinade and pat dry. Heat the oil in heavy-based frying pan and sear the beef well on all sides. Remove from the pan, place in a large roasting tin and roast for 25 minutes in the preheated oven. Test for doneness with a sharp knife. Allow the meat to rest for 10 minutes before carving.

5 Carve the meat in 1 cm (½ in) slices. Place on a warm serving platter with dollops or bowls of the coriander-peanut pesto.

diva**dos**

 Beef sirloin can replace fillet.

 The coriander and peanut pesto can be made the day before.

 The beef can be served hot or cold. Serve with Caramelized New Potatoes or Baby Green Salad (see pages 136 and 135). Garnish with strips of spring onion, chilli, coriander leaves or toasted sesame seeds.

diva**don'ts**

 Don't hesitate to remove the meat from the oven before it is cooked to your liking, as it will continue to 'cook' when resting.

diva**birds**

braised duck legs with soy, ginger and star anise

● Serves: 8 ● Preparation: 15 minutes ● Cooking: 1½ hours

Duck is forever glamorous. This is an excellent do-ahead party dish, that will fill your home with fragrant aromas.

8 duck legs

4 tbsp runny honey

1 tsp Chinese five-spice powder

5 garlic cloves, sliced

6 cm (2½ in) piece fresh root ginger, cut into strips

250 ml (9 fl oz) chicken stock

5 tbsp saké

125 ml (4 fl oz) red wine

125 ml (4 fl oz) light soy sauce

4 star anise

garnish

½ bunch of spring onions

2 red chillies, seeded

1 Preheat the oven to 180°C/ 350°F/Gas 4.

2 Trim the excess fat from under the duck legs. Brown the legs in a hot frying pan with no oil. Place in a large roasting tray, and drizzle with the honey and sprinkle over the five-spice powder.

3 Tip out any duck fat from the frying pan, then add the garlic and ginger, and sauté for 2 minutes. Add all the liquids and the star anise, bring to the boil and simmer for 5 minutes.

4 Pour the ginger liquid around the duck, and tightly seal with foil, ensuring there are no holes or rips. Roast in the preheated oven for an hour. Remove the foil and increase the oven to 220°C/425°F/Gas 7. Cook for another 15 minutes to crisp the skin (or place under a hot grill).

5 To serve, place the duck legs on a warm platter. Discard any fat from the juices and spoon the remaining juices around the duck. Garnish with the spring onions and chilli, both cut into julienne strips.

diva**dos**

Some duck legs are juicer than others; we use Gressingham.

The duck can be cooked well ahead, and kept covered with foil. To reheat, place into the oven at 180°C/350°F/Gas 4 for 15 minutes, then remove the foil and cook for another 15 minutes. If the juices start to dry up, add some boiling water, bring to the boil and whisk to combine the juices.

Be careful when crisping the duck not to burn the juices.

We serve with a chicory, watercress, red onion and pear salad, lightly tossed in lemon juice and olive oil.

guinea fowl breasts with tarragon and crème fraîche

● Serves: 8   ● Preparation: 15 minutes   ● Cooking: 30 minutes

A French classic, which has been given a make-over – seared, tender guinea fowl in a creamy tart sauce, enlivened with fresh tarragon.

8 guinea fowl breasts

25 g (1 oz) butter

1 tsp each of salt and pepper

20 large shallots, roughly sliced

250 ml (9 fl oz) tarragon vinegar

125 ml (4 fl oz) white wine

90 ml (3 fl oz) chicken stock

2 bunches of fresh tarragon, stems removed, leaves chopped

125 ml (4 fl oz) crème fraîche

1 Melt the butter in a deep, large saucepan, and brown the guinea fowl on both sides. Sprinkle with salt and pepper, and remove from the pan.

2 Sauté the shallots in the same pan until soft and golden. Add the vinegar and boil to reduce by half.

3 Place the guinea fowl back in the saucepan. Add the wine, stock and half the chopped tarragon. Cook

uncovered over a low heat for 20–30 minutes or until the guinea fowl is tender. Add the crème fraîche and remaining tarragon just before serving.

4 Serve with basmati or long-grain white rice.

diva**dos**

 Ask your butcher to bone the guinea fowl, but to leave a decorative wing bone. You can use other poultry, like chicken thighs and breasts.

 This recipe freezes well and can be made a day ahead to reheat (at 160°C/325°F/Gas 3)

 Start the evening off with Sun-blush Tomato Pesto with Pitta Breadsticks (see page 11), and serve with Baby Green Salad with Classic Vinaigrette (see pages 135 and 118).

diva**don'ts**

 Don't let the dish boil hard once the crème fraîche has been added or it may separate.

korean barbecued chicken with cucumber salad

● Serves: 8   ● Preparation: 2 hours marinating plus 30 minutes   ● Cooking: 15 minutes

Korean food is relatively unfamiliar. Sweet, sour and spicy, lots of garlic and sesame oil are the quintessential flavours. Marinated grilled chicken is wrapped in crunchy lettuce and served with a spicy cucumber salad.

16 boneless, skinless chicken thighs

16 lettuce leaves (iceberg or cos)

marinade

8 tbsp Korean sweet-spicy chilli paste (kochujang)

175 ml (6 fl oz) saké or mirin

3 tbsp light soy sauce

3 tbsp crushed garlic

3 tbsp sesame salt

4 tbsp sesame oil

3 tbsp grated fresh root ginger

2 tbsp pepper

1 tbsp salt

6 spring onions, finely sliced

cucumber salad

2 small cucumbers, seeded (if large, then use 1)

4 tbsp rice wine vinegar

1 tsp each of salt and pepper

1 tbsp caster sugar

1 tsp dried crushed red chilli

1 Mix all the marinade ingredients together. Pour over the chicken and leave refrigerated for at least 2 hours, but preferably for a day or overnight.

2 For the salad, thinly slice or julienne the cucumbers. Mix the remaining ingredients and pour over, cover and refrigerate for at least half an hour before serving the chicken.

3 Place the chicken under a hot, pre-heated grill or on a barbecue, for about 10 minutes each side, or until cooked.

4 Serve the chicken on a platter with the lettuce on the side. Guests can bundle their chicken in the lettuce and top with the cucumber salad before wrapping.

diva**dos**

 Look for kochujang in a Japanese or Asian grocery, or try one of the new internet sites for ethnic foods. Substitute another chilli paste if you cannot get it.

 Marinate the chicken the night before as this saves time on the day of the party.

 Serve the chicken on a large white platter decorated with more spring onion or coriander leaves. Simplicity is best for Asian food. Serve with other Asian favourites, like Thai Green Papaya Salad with Seared Chilli Prawns or Tamarind-roasted Vegetables (see pages 120 and 128).

brochettes of lemon chicken, sage, and croûtons with red pepper aïoli

● Serves: 8   ● Preparation: 30 minutes marinating plus 1 hour   ● Cooking: 15 minutes

A wondrous myriad of flavours and textures from Tuscany, perfect for a summer picnic. You will need 16 wooden skewers, which you should soak in water for an hour beforehand.

6 boneless, skinless chicken breasts

12 slices of prosciutto, each cut into 4 strips

½ French stick

32 sage leaves

3 garlic cloves, finely chopped

juice and grated zest of 1 large, juicy lemon

salt and pepper

4 tbsp olive oil

red pepper aïoli

1 red pepper, quartered and seeded

250 ml (9 fl oz) Classic Mayonnaise (see page 118)

3 garlic cloves

juice of 1 lemon

15 g (½ oz) basil

1 To make the aïoli, place the pepper quarters under a very hot grill, skin side up, and grill until the skin has blackened. Remove and place in a bag to cool. Peel the pepper, discarding the skin. Place with all the remaining aïoli ingredients in a food processor, and puree until smooth. Taste for seasoning. Keep chilled until ready to serve.

2 Cut the chicken into 48 equal chunks. Wrap each chunk in a slice of prosciutto.

3 Cut the bread into 32 equal-sized chunks. Thread on to each skewer a piece of chicken, a sage leaf, a chunk of bread, followed by chicken, then sage and bread, finishing with a piece of chicken. Repeat this process for all 16 skewers.

4 Mix together the garlic, lemon juice, zest, salt and pepper with the olive oil, and brush liberally over the brochettes. Leave to marinate for 30 minutes.

5 Preheat a large griddle, frying pan, grill or barbecue. Sear the chicken for 5 minutes on each side, for a total of 15 minutes.

diva**dos**

Chicken thigh can be used instead. You can use rosemary skewers instead (see page 20).

The brochettes can be assembled the day before, covered and chilled. Marinate them up to an hour beforehand. The aïoli can be made 2 days before, covered and chilled.

Arrange the chicken on a large serving platter, with sprigs of herbs and a large bowl of the aïoli. Serve with Saffron-roasted potatoes or Fennel Slaw (see pages 138 and 134).

diva**don'ts**

Don't use stainless-steel cutlery when making or serving the aïoli, or it will take on a metallic flavour. Use wooden or silver spoons.

seared duck breasts with balsamic vinegar, rosemary and shallot sauce

● Serves: 8 ● Preparation: 1 hour marinating plus 15 minutes ● Cooking: 30 minutes

We made this years ago at the Books for Cooks Valentine's Day dinner. It was such a success that we had to include it in the book.

8 duck breasts

marinade

1 tbsp clear honey

2 tbsp light soy sauce

salt and pepper

balsamic, rosemary and shallot sauce

1 tbsp olive oil

6 shallots, finely sliced

2 tbsp chopped rosemary

150 ml (5 fl oz) red wine

250 ml (9 fl oz) balsamic vinegar

175 ml (6 fl oz) chicken stock

1–2 tbsp fruit jelly, such as crab-apple or elderberry

55 g (2 oz) butter, chilled and diced

1 Preheat the oven to 190°C/ 375°F/Gas 5.

2 Trim any excess fat from the duck breasts. Mix together the marinade ingredients, pour over the duck and leave for 1 hour.

3 Heat a heavy frying pan, add the duck and brown well on both sides. Remove from the pan, place in a roasting tray and roast in the preheated oven for 10–15 minutes until still pink. Allow to rest for 5 minutes before carving.

4 To make the sauce, heat the olive oil in a saucepan. Wilt the shallots and rosemary, cooking until caramelised, about 10 minutes. Add the wine and balsamic vinegar, bring to the boil and reduce to an eighth. Add the stock and reduce by half. Whisk in the fruit jelly, simmer for 5 minutes and then bring back to the boil. Whisk in the chilled butter to thicken and enrich the sauce.

5 Serve the duck sliced on warm plates with the sauce.

diva**dos**

 We use Gressingham duck breasts. Do not use cheap balsamic vinegar, as it will affect the taste of the sauce. Redcurrant jelly works well but does have quite a strong flavour.

 Marinate the duck the day before. The sauce can be made earlier in the day, but do not add the butter until reheating to serve.

 We serve it with Sweet Potato and Ginger Mash (see page 130), a roasted pumpkin puree or French beans tossed in toasted sesame seeds and light soy sauce.

 You can sear the duck hours before, then roast in the hot oven at the last minute. Allow to rest for 10 minutes.

balsamic chicken with porcini mushrooms and sun-dried cherries

● Serves: 8   ● Preparation: 30 minutes   ● Cooking: 45 minutes

This elegant braised chicken is the perfect make-ahead meal. Porcini mushrooms, balsamic vinegar and dried cherries are a divine combination. Serve with any vegetable mash for a great winter meal.

55 g (2 oz) dried porcini mushrooms

8 large boneless, skinless chicken thighs

4 tbsp plain flour

1 tsp each of salt and pepper

250 g (9 oz) pancetta bacon, diced, or smoked bacon, chopped

1 olive oil

2 onions, finely chopped

6 garlic cloves, finely chopped

20 dried cherries, roughly chopped

125 ml (4 fl oz) balsamic vinegar

500 ml (18 fl oz) red wine

250 ml (9 fl oz) chicken stock

1 tsp arrowroot or cornflour, dissolved in 2 tsp cold water

a handful of flat-leaf parsley, chopped (about 15 g (½ oz)

1 Pour 250 ml (9 fl oz) boiling water over the porcini mushrooms. Leave for half an hour, then carefully strain through a fine sieve, reserving the liquid. Roughly chop the porcini.

2 Dredge the chicken in seasoned flour and set aside. Fry the pancetta in a little olive oil until it is very crisp. Remove from the pan and set aside. Brown the chicken pieces on both sides in the bacon fat. Remove from the pan, then sauté the onions and garlic until soft.

3 Stir the porcini mushrooms into the onion along with the cherries, vinegar, red wine, stock and reserved porcini liquid. Bring to the boil and simmer for 10 minutes.

4 Add the chicken and pancetta, bring to a simmer and cook for 30 minutes. Add the arrowroot or cornflour mixture and simmer for another 5 minutes. Check for additional salt or balsamic vinegar.

diva**dos**

Make this dish the night before to save time and improve the intensity of flavours.

Serve with any type of white mash or puree. Celeriac, potatoes or Jerusalem artichokes are all yummy possibilities. Start with Spiedini of Scallops or Grilled Red Peppers (see pages 87 and 106).

diva**don'ts**

Don't use poor-quality balsamic vinegar – splash out on superior brands, like Fini.

birds

Poultry is probably the most widely eaten meat in the world. Because of its mild flavours, it can be enhanced with zesty marinades and sauces or simply paired with fresh herbs. On a hot summer day there is nothing like the taste of barbecued chicken with crispy skin. Duck is the favourite for more formal events, turkey is for holidays and chicken for ethnic and casual meals. We recommend organic, corn-fed or free-range chickens for their taste and texture.

DUCK

Duck Legs: These are best known for their role in the classic French confit. Not only are duck legs inexpensive, but the meat is tender and flaky when braised. Asian flavours such as soy sauce, garlic, chillies, ginger, and spring onion are excellent baked with legs. Mediterranean ingredients such as balsamic vinegar, thyme, prunes, and olives are also fantastic additions. As duck can be quite fatty, cut off excess fat and sear the portions, skin side down, to render the fat. The liquid fat can then be drained off before braising. For large duck pieces, buy Barbary duck legs, and for smaller portions, purchase Gressingham.

Duck Breasts: The most prized part of duck, breasts are perfect for an elegant occasion. Purchase the smaller Gressingham birds, which are lean and full of flavour, or female Barbary, which are far smaller than the male ducks. Because the fat is so thick on the breasts, trim off any overlapping fat and score the skin in a diamond pattern, using a sharp knife, to help it render the fat when searing. Marinating the breasts before cooking helps to keep them juicy as they can sometimes be dry. Port, red wine, balsamic vinegar, soy sauce, honey, and pomegranate molasses are just a few of the flavours that they combine with best. You can also include spices such as juniper berries, roasted cumin seeds, and star anise. To cook, preheat a heavy, dry frying pan, sear the duck for several minutes on both sides, then place the duck in a hot oven and roast for 10 minutes until pink. Allow the meat to rest for 5 minutes in a warm place before slicing. Duck breasts can also be grilled or barbecued.

Wild Duck: Wild duck is a real game-lover's treat. It's available from your butcher or game dealer from early September until late January to mid-February. The most common varieties are teal, mallard and widgeon – but which to choose? Well, here's a quick guide: the mallard (a relation of the farmyard duck) is an omnivorous bird, so we would rather recommend the widgeon, which feeds only on grass, and is famed for its excellent flavour. The tiny teal is also a little gem, especially if there aren't many mouths to feed! Make sure you reserve the carcass to make a deliciously rich, gamey stock, which will enhance any winter sauce beyond your expectations!

To make the most of your wild duck breast, we recommend marinating it overnight with crushed juniper berries, a little honey and some port. The wild duck can then be seared and roasted by following the same methods employed in other duck recipes (see pages 38, 68 and 74). Try serving the breast with our Balsamic Vinegar, Rosemary and Shallot Sauce (see page 74), or any other sauce that you would normally serve with duck.

To make the duck stock (this method works equally well with all game birds), begin by placing the carcass in a large stock pot with a couple of chopped onions, carrots, mushrooms, bay leaves, 6 black peppercorns and a parsley stalk. Cover and bring to the boil, then reduce the heat immediately, and simmer for two hours, regularly skimming the stock. Next, strain the stock and discard the carcass and all other ingredients, keeping just the liquid. Pour the liquid into a clean pan and reduce by half over a high heat – this will create a fuller more concentrated, more satisfying flavour! Cool the stock and decant – you can then either chill in the fridge for two days before use, or freeze. Wild duck stores extremely well, and like all poultry can be frozen for up to six months so it can be enjoyed out of season! When freezing, it's very important to ensure that the meat is well-wrapped and labelled to avoid confusion or damaging the texture or flavours!

CHICKEN

Chicken Thighs: Virtually all the supermarkets are now selling boneless chicken thighs. We think they're the best-kept secret in town. They're far cheaper than breasts, juicier and great value for money. Be sure and cut off the excess fat on them before cooking. Boneless chicken thighs are fantastic for skewering, barbecues, stews, and pan-frying. Almost any flavour can be used with them – Moroccan, South-East Asian, Middle Eastern, Mediterranean, or Japanese. They are superb if marinated before cooking in anything from garlic and olive oil to Korean sweet spicy chilli paste or kochujang (see page 71).

Chicken Breasts: The breast meat can be pan-fried or grilled for a casual gathering, as well as char-grilled, stuffed and sliced for lavish dinners. Careful thought must be given to how chicken breasts are cooked to keep them nice and juicy – they can become rubbery and dry. Marinating in vinaigrettes, yogurts, coconut milk, Asian sauces, or citrus juice is highly recommended to keep them juicy. They are best served with very gusty sauces such as salsa verde, sweet chilli sauce, spicy chilli salsas, or charmoula. Poaching chicken breast works well – cool chicken in the poaching water, then shred or slice chicken to use.

Guinea Fowl: This bird is very similar to chicken but darker in colour and with a slightly gamier taste. Guineau fowl are becoming increasingly popular. They are well suited to French Provençal flavours such as tarragon, crème fraîche, bacon, thyme, olives, and garlic. With a tendency to dryness, guinea fowl needs careful cooking and should be basted frequently or prepared with a sauce to prevent drying out. Supremes, which are a breast cut with the wing bone attached at the top, are especially good for parties. Ask your butcher to prepare them for you. The wing bone serves no other purpose than looking elegant. (You could also remove the bones and use them to make an excellent stock.)

Poussin: These are four- to six-week old baby chickens, and they are absolutely lovely to barbecue and grill. They are best prepared by a process known as spatchcocking, which is removing the backbone, flattening and securing with metal skewers. This helps the tiny birds to cook evenly and quickly. They benefit from marinating overnight to help keep the flesh moist. Thai, Chinese and Mediterranean marinades all produce delicious results. A poussin generally serves one person, but if including with other dishes as part of a meal, allow half a bird per head.

grilled indonesian coconut chicken

● Serves: 8 ● Preparation: 4 hours marinating plus 20 minutes ● Cooking: 20 minutes

The Indonesians have a genius for marinating with big flavours. The aroma of the lemongrass, ginger and garlic will drive your guests mad. This recipe is excellent for summer, when barbecuing is at its height.

16 boneless, skinless chicken thighs

fresh coriander leaves

marinade

4 lemongrass stalks, outer leaves discarded, root ends trimmed

a large handful of fresh coriander, chopped

6 shallots, sliced

8 large garlic cloves, peeled

fresh root ginger, chopped

4 tbsp brown sugar

2 tbsp curry powder

2 tsp pepper

½ tsp salt

4 tbsp Thai fish sauce (nam pla)

400 ml (14 fl oz) coconut milk

1 Finely chop the lower 15 cm (6 in) of the lemongrass stalks, discarding the remainder of the stalks, then slice. In a food processor finely grind together the lemongrass, coriander, shallots, garlic and ginger. Add the sugar, curry powder, pepper, salt, fish sauce and coconut milk, and blend to a puree.

2 Place the chicken in a suitable container. Pour the marinade over the chicken, covering well. Chill overnight or for at least 4 hours. Remember to turn once or twice.

3 Preheat an overhead grill or barbecue, or set the oven to its highest temperature.

4 Grill or roast the chicken in its marinade for 20 minutes, turning over once to caramelise. Serve the chicken on a large platter sprinkled with coriander leaves.

diva**dos**

 Cut excess fat off the chicken thighs as well as the skin.

 Marinate 24 hours ahead for perfect flavour and time saved on the day.

 We suggest serving with white rice, but as part of a Asian menu, serve with Thai Beef Salad and Green Papaya Salad with Seared Chilli Prawns (see pages 126 and 120).

diva**don'ts**

 Don't overcook barbecuing, as the chicken will quickly dry out.

smoky chipotle chicken with pineapple salsa

● Serves: 8   ● Preparation: 1 hour   ● Cooking: 15 minutes

Discovering chipotle chillies is one of life's greatest treats. They impart a spicy smoky flavour to any dish, but use them sparingly as they are powerfully hot.

8 large boneless, skinless chicken thighs, trimmed of all fat, or 6 chicken breasts, skinless

2 tbsp groundnut oil

7–8 ripe plum tomatoes, halved

8 garlic cloves, unpeeled

2–3 chipotle chillies in adobo sauce, or dried chillies, rehydrated in water (seeds and stems removed)

a small handful of fresh coriander

salt and pepper

1 large onion, chopped

3 tbsp vegetable oil

grilled pineapple salsa

2 tbsp vegetable oil

1 fresh pineapple, peeled and cut into slices

juice of 3 limes

1 large red onion, chopped

20 g (¾ oz) fresh coriander, chopped

to serve

16 flour tortillas

crème fraîche

fresh coriander leaves

1 Pan-fry the chicken thighs slowly in the oil until they are browned and cooked through. Chop or shred while hot.

2 Blacken the tomatoes on both sides under a hot grill. Place the garlic in a non-stick saucepan, and blacken both sides over a medium heat. Cool and peel. Roughly puree the tomatoes, garlic, chipotles, the fresh coriander, salt and pepper in a food processor.

3 Sauté the chopped onion in the oil in a saucepan. Add the shredded chicken and stir-fry for 10 minutes. Pour the tomato puree over and cook to thicken for about 5 minutes.

4 Preheat a char-grill pan or barbecue. Brush oil on the pineapple pieces and grill on both sides until black lines appear. Remove and cut out the round core in each piece. Roughly chop the pineapple and combine with the remaining salsa ingredients and some salt and pepper.

5 Prepare the wraps by heaping 4 tbsp of the warm chicken into the centre of each tortilla. Top with 2 tbsp pineapple salsa and 1 tsp crème fraîche. Fold the bottom of the tortilla up about 2.5 cm (1 in) and fold the sides over. Leave the top open and sprinkle with coriander leaves. Serve immediately.

diva**dos**

 Buy a tin of chipotle chillies in adobo sauce, found at speciality markets or by mail order, and keep covered in an airtight container. They will last for at least 6 months.

 Cook the shredded chicken the day before and chill. Prepare the salsa on the morning of the party.

 Serve on a platter decorated with grilled lime halves and loads of fresh coriander. Start the evening off with Spiced Corn Cakes or Tuna Ceviche (see pages 17 and 32) and their respective salsas.

diva**don'ts**

 Don't use green pineapples – look for firm ones with a golden colour.

seared thai chicken with tomato-chilli jam

● Serves: 8 ● Preparation: 1 hour marinating plus 25 minutes ● Cooking: 45 minutes

Simply marinated chicken paired with a sweet and piquant chilli jam. It's possibly one of our all-time favourites.

8 boneless, skinless chicken breasts

marinade

4 tbsp sesame oil

4 tbsp Thai fish sauce (nam pla)

1 tbsp clear honey

3 garlic cloves, chopped

2 red chillies, seeded and finely chopped

25 g (1 oz) fresh coriander, finely chopped

tomato-chilli jam

500 g (1 lb 2 oz) ripe tomatoes, chopped

4 red chillies, seeded and chopped

4 garlic cloves

5 cm (2 in) piece of fresh root ginger, chopped

2 tbsp Thai fish sauce (nam pla)

300 g (10½ oz) soft brown sugar

100 ml (3½ fl oz) red wine vinegar

3 Thai lime leaves

55 g (2 oz) raisins

1 To make the tomato-chilli jam, place half the tomatoes, the chilli, garlic, ginger and fish sauce in a food processor and blend to a puree. Place this puree in a heavy-based saucepan with the sugar, vinegar, lime leaves and raisins, and bring to the boil slowly, stirring. Chop the remaining tomatoes into small dice and add to the jam once it has come to the boil. Simmer gently for 45 minutes, stirring occasionally. If the tomatoes are very watery it may need longer, but the jam will thicken when cold.

2 Slice the chicken into thick strips. Mix the marinade ingredients together, pour over the chicken, cover and chill for 1 hour or up to 1 day.

3 Preheat a large griddle, frying pan or barbecue. Sear the chicken for 5 minutes on each side, brushing with the marinade as it cooks.

4 Serve hot or cold. If serving hot, keep warm in a medium oven until ready to eat. Pile on to a large serving plate alongside bowls of chilli jam.

diva**dos**

 Use chicken thighs instead. If time is short, bottled Thai sweet chilli sauce is an excellent substitute for the jam.

 Make the jam a month ahead and keep chilled in a screw-top jar. The chicken can be marinated the day before the event.

 We often serve this chicken on wooden skewers, which makes great party fare. It is best cooked to serve, but you can cook 30 minutes before and keep warm in a medium oven. Serve with large lime wedges, coriander and we sometimes scatter it with toasted sesame seeds. Sweet Potato and Ginger Mash, Fragrant Coconut Rice or Tamarind-roasted Vegetables (see pages 130, 139 and 128) are the ideal accompaniments to this dish.

diva**fish**

grilled prawns with tamarind recado and pineapple and red onion salsa

• Serves: 8   • Preparation: 30 minutes marinating and 1 hour   • Cooking: 5 minutes

Prawns taste fabulous marinated and basted with recado, a spicy, sweet and sour Mexican marinade. Here the recado is prepared with gorgeous tamarind, which makes a lovely glaze.

40 large raw prawns, peeled

tamarind recado

125 g (4½ oz) tamarind pulp (in a sticky block) or 300 g (10½ oz) bottled tamarind puree

350 ml (12 fl oz) boiling water

10 garlic cloves, unpeeled

1 onion, thickly sliced

4 plum tomatoes, halved

3 dried chipotle chillies, in adobe sauce, or 3 dried chillies, rehydrated in water (stemmed and seeded)

1 tbsp salt

2 tbsp brown sugar

salsa

500 ml (18 fl oz) coarsely chopped fresh pineapple

1 red onion, finely chopped

a large handful of fresh coriander, chopped

juice of 2 limes

salt and pepper

1 To make the recado, place the tamarind pulp in a bowl and pour over the boiling water. Leave to soak until soft and fairly liquid. Pour through a sieve and set aside. (Or use the bottled tamarind puree instead) Place the garlic in a hot, dry frying pan and cook over a high heat until softened and charred. Cool, then peel. Preheat a hot grill, place the onions and tomatoes underneath until blackened.

2 Place the tamarind liquid, chillies, onion, tomatoes, garlic, salt and sugar in a food processor and blend until smooth.

3 Coat the prawns with the recado in a shallow dish, cover, and leave to marinate in the fridge for 30 minutes to 1 hour. Soak bamboo skewers in water for at least 30 minutes.

4 Mix the salsa ingredients together and season to taste.

5 Thread the prawns on to the skewers and grill or barbecue for 5 minutes, basting with remaining marinade during cooking. Serve with the salsa.

diva**dos**

 Buy tamarind pulp from an Indian or Thai shop, or bottled tamarind from large supermarkets.

 The recado can be made up to 12 days ahead. Make the salsa on the day of serving.

 The prawns look fantastic served on banana leaves, garnished with coriander sprigs and lime wedges.

diva**don'ts**

 Don't be mean and buy anorexic prawns. Get king-size prawns – they will be worth it.

 Take care not to overcook the prawns, as they will become tough and rubbery.

spicy crab cakes with cherry tomato and coriander salsa

● Makes: 16   ● Preparation: 45 minutes   ● Cooking: 20 minutes

These crispy crab cakes work well served as a starter or main course or can be made smaller, canapé-size, to serve a crowd.

crab cakes

350 g (12 oz) white crabmeat, well drained

1 red onion, finely chopped

2 tbsp runny honey

1 tsp crushed dried red chillies

250 g (9 oz) fresh breadcrumbs

250 ml (9 fl oz) Classic Mayonnaise (see page 118)

1 egg

25 g (1 oz) fresh coriander, finely chopped

salt and cayenne pepper

grated zest and juice of 2 limes

1 tsp Tabasco sauce

125 ml (4 fl oz) sunflower or groundnut oil

cherry tomato and coriander salsa

4 spring onions, finely chopped

15 g (½ oz) fresh coriander, chopped

250 g (9 oz) ripe cherry tomatoes, quartered

2 red chillies, seeded and finely chopped

1 tbsp Thai fish sauce

juice of 1 lime

the garnish

baby salad leaves or rocket

lime wedges

1 Place all the crab cake ingredients except the oil in a large bowl and mix together. Shape the mixture into 16 even-sized cakes and chill.

2 To make the salsa, mix all the ingredients together and season to taste.

3 Heat a little of the oil in a large, heavy-based frying pan. Cook the crab cakes in batches over a medium heat for about 2 minutes on each side, using a fish slice to turn them over. Add extra oil as needed. Keep the crab cakes warm in a moderate oven.

4 Serve on a bed of salad leaves, garnished with lime wedges and little bowls of the salsa.

diva**dos**

 You can use canned white crab or fresh crabmeat.

 The crab cakes can be made the day before serving and kept chilled in the fridge. Make the salsa up to 6 hours ahead, but do not add the seasoning, fish sauce or lime juice until 30 minutes before serving.

 The crab cakes can be fried 1 hour before serving and kept warm in a moderate oven.

 Serve as a starter before Roast Fillet of Beef with Coriander and Peanut Pesto or as a main course with Parsley and Roasted Garlic Tart and Fennel Slaw (see pages 66, 38 and 134). Creme fraiche is also delicious with the crab cakes.

fennel and seafood bouillabaisse with saffron aïoli

● Serves: 8   ● Preparation: 50 minutes   ● Cooking: 30 minutes

An extremely elegant soup, perfect for a special occasion.

soup

2 tbsp olive oil

3 garlic cloves, finely chopped

2 onions, finely chopped

1 fennel bulb, finely chopped

2 carrots, finely chopped

1 potato, peeled and chopped

150 ml (5 fl oz) dry white wine

900 ml (1½ pints) fish stock

3 tomatoes, seeded and chopped

juice of 1 lemon

salt and cayenne pepper

500 g (1 lb 2 oz) monkfish tail, skinned
and sliced into thick pieces

8 king scallops, trimmed

16 raw king prawns, peeled

chopped fresh dill to garnish

saffron aïoli

2 pinches of saffron threads

2 tbsp boiling water

2 egg yolks

3 garlic cloves, finely chopped

juice of 1 lemon

1 tsp Dijon mustard

½ tsp sugar

300 ml (10 fl oz) sunflower oil

1 To make the aïoli, place the saffron in a small bowl, pour over the water and leave for 5 minutes. Place the egg yolks, garlic, lemon juice, mustard and sugar in a food processor. Slowly drizzle in the oil and blend to form a thick, creamy mayonnaise. Add the saffron liquid, season to taste, then chill.

2 For the soup, heat the olive oil in a large saucepan, add the garlic and vegetables and cook gently for 5 minutes until softened. Add the wine, then the stock and tomatoes. Bring to the boil, then reduce the heat, cover and simmer for 20 minutes. Add lemon juice and seasoning.

3 Just before serving, add the fish to the simmering soup and cook gently for 5 minutes until just tender. The prawns will turn pink. Serve in warmed bowls, sprinkled with dill. Pass the aïoli in a bowl separately for guests to spoon on to their soup.

diva**dos**

 Alternative fish may be added, such as cod, baby squid or lobster.

 This is an excellent party dish, as the aïoli and the vegetable broth can be made well ahead.

 Add the fish to the broth just before serving, to keep it tender.

 Serve as an elegant starter or hearty main course, with the vegetables and fish cut into larger chunks. Serve with Miniature Focaccia or Diva Breadsticks (see pages 161 and 158).

spiedini of scallops with a chunky salsa verde

● Serves: 8 ● Preparation: 25 minutes ● Cooking: 10 minutes

Once you experience salsa verde, you can become seriously addicted! Not only is it packed with flavour, it's healthy and simple to make. We've updated it slightly with crunchy red onion for more texture. Delicate scallops make the perfect partner. Allow 3 scallops each as a starter or 4 each for a main course.

8 x 25 cm (10 in) rosemary sprigs

24–32 king scallops, shelled

2 tbsp olive oil

juice of 1 lemon

salsa verde

1 large bunch of flat-leaf parsley

1 bunch of basil leaves

10–15 mint leaves

2 garlic cloves, peeled

2 anchovies, rinsed

2 tbsp capers, rinsed

3 tbsp red wine vinegar

1 tsp mustard

salt and pepper

175 ml (6 fl oz) extra virgin olive oil

1 small red onion, finely diced

1 Take the rosemary sprigs and pull off most of the needles, leaving just the needles at the top, to make herb skewers. Sprinkle the scallops with olive oil, salt and pepper. Thread 3–4 scallops onto each rosemary sprig. Chill until ready to cook.

2 Place all the ingredients for the salsa verde in a food processor, except the olive oil and red onion.

Pulse until the mixture is roughly chopped. Slowly add the oil until it is all incorporated. Scrape into a bowl and add the red onion.

3 Preheat a heavy sauté pan. Add the scallop skewers in batches and sear for 1 minute on each side. Squeeze over the lemon juice. Serve on a large platter and accompany with the salsa verde.

diva**dos**

 Leave the orange muscle on the side of the scallops – it's very tasty. Raid your neighbours' gardens for large sprigs of rosemary – the supermarket variety won't be long or strong enough.

 You can make the salsa verde the day before. Keep it covered and chilled. Thread the scallops on to the rosemary skewers on the morning of the party.

 If cooking for a large number, sear the scallops quickly in advance and allow to cool. Later, preheat the oven to 200°C/400°F/Gas 6. Just before serving, roast the scallops in the oven for 5 minutes.

 Serve with Grilled Red Peppers stuffed with Herbed Ricotta or Tuscan Panzanella Salad (see pages 106 and 123) for the ultimate Mediterranean feast.

diva**don'ts**

 Take care not to overcook the scallops, as they will shrink and lose their precious juices.

prawn dumplings in fragrant thai broth

- Serves: 8 regular servings or 6 greedy ones   • Preparation: 30 minutes
- Cooking: 30 minutes

Delicate prawn dumplings in a tasty coconut broth make this a meal in itself.
The ingenious ingredient, tom yum paste, which is the Thai equivalent to stock
cubes, provides a wonderful sweet, spicy and sour flavour.

prawn dumplings

1 garlic clove, peeled

2.5 cm (1 in) piece of fresh root ginger

2 shallots, peeled

225 g (8 oz) raw prawns, peeled

1 egg white

1 tsp cornflour

2 tbsp chopped fresh coriander

salt and pepper

stock

prawn shells and heads (optional)

2 chunks of fresh root ginger,
peeled and chopped

6 garlic cloves, sliced

a large handful of fresh coriander
stalks, chopped

coconut broth

400 ml can coconut milk

100 g (3½ oz) tom yum paste

4 lime leaves, finely chopped

2 tbsp Thai fish sauce (nam pla)

juice of 2 limes

125 g (4½ oz) fresh shiitake
mushrooms, thinly sliced

125 g (4½ oz) baby corn,
sliced in half lengthways

15 g (½ oz) basil leaves, torn

fresh coriander leaves to garnish

1 To make the dumplings, place
the garlic, ginger and shallots in
a food processor, and pulse until
finely chopped. Add the prawns,
egg white, cornflour, coriander and
seasoning. Puree to a rough paste.
Chill until needed.

2 For the stock, heat 3 litres (5¼
pints) water in a large saucepan.
Add the prawn shells and heads, if
using, the ginger, garlic and coriander
stalks. Bring to the boil, then reduce
the heat and simmer for 20 minutes.
Sieve and discard the solids.

3 Pour the stock back into the pan
and add the coconut milk, tom yum
paste, lime leaves, fish sauce and

lime juice. Bring back to the boil,
then simmer for 5 minutes. Season
to taste.

4 Five minutes before serving, add
the mushrooms and baby corn to
the soup.

5 Using a teaspoon, shape the
prawn mixture into little balls and drop
into the simmering soup. Cook for
3–4 minutes until they float to the
top. Add basil.

6 Ladle into bowls and garnish with
coriander leaves.

diva**dos**

 *Buy tom yum paste from your Thai
grocer or large supermarkets.
Once opened, it will keep for ages
in the fridge. If unavailable, replace
with 2 fish or tom yum stock
cubes. Do buy unpeeled prawns –
the shells really enhance the flavour
of the stock.*

 *You can prepare the soup and
the dumpling mixture the day
before serving.*

 *Serve the soup in Asian ceramic
bowls – very Diva! Serve with Thai
Green Papaya Salad with Seared
Chilli Prawns or Soba Noodle Salad
(see pages 120 and 119).*

sweet potato, prawn, and ginger fritters with cucumber relish

● Makes: 16   ● Preparation: 20 minutes   ● Cooking: 15 minutes

Crunchy fritters with succulent prawns, topped off with a refreshing cucumber relish. Yum!

fritters

75 g (2¾ oz) plain flour

3 medium eggs, separated

1 tsp salt

a large pinch of cayenne pepper

400 g (14 oz) sweet potato, grated

3 spring onions, finely chopped

2.5 cm (1 in) piece of fresh root ginger, peeled and grated

15 g (½ oz) fresh coriander, finely chopped

16 raw king prawns, peeled

4 tbsp groundnut oil

cucumber relish

125 ml (4 fl oz) rice wine vinegar

2 tbsp caster sugar

1 carrot, finely chopped

2 shallots, finely chopped

2.5 cm (1 in) piece of cucumber, seeded and finely chopped

1 red chilli, seeded and finely chopped (or ½ tsp crushed dried red chilli)

15 g (½ oz) fresh coriander, chopped

grated zest and juice of 1 lime

1 Place the flour, egg yolks, 125 ml (4 fl oz) cold water, salt and cayenne pepper in a bowl and mix to a smooth paste. Stir in the sweet potato, spring onions, ginger and coriander. Whisk the egg whites until stiff, then fold into the mixture to make a batter.

2 Slice the prawns in half lengthways. Heat 4 tbsp of the oil in a non-stick frying pan. Take 1 tbsp of the fritter batter and push in 2 prawn halves. Slide the fritter into the hot oil and fry for 2 minutes on each side,

until golden and crispy. Repeat with the remaining mixture and prawns, adding more oil if needed. Keep the fritters warm until ready to serve.

3 To make the relish, gently heat the vinegar and sugar in a saucepan until the sugar has dissolved. Bring to the boil, then boil for a few minutes until syrupy. Remove from the heat, allow to cool, then add the remaining relish ingredients. Adjust the seasoning if necessary. Serve with the fritters.

diva**dos**

 If tight for time, you could use bottled Thai chilli dipping sauce to serve in place of the relish.

 The relish vegetables can be chopped and chilled the day before, but the relish should be finished on the day of serving. Add more chilli if you like spicy food. The batter for the fritters can be made (without adding the egg whites) up to 2 hours before serving and kept chilled. Add the beaten egg whites just before frying.

 The fritters can be cooked up to 30 minutes before serving, then kept warm.

 Serve the fritters hot on a large white platter, garnished with coriander sprigs and lime wedges with the relish in small dipping bowls. Serve the fritters with Korean Barbecue Chicken or Vietnamese Minced Chicken Salad (see pages 71 and 115).

fish

Fish is not only quick to prepare, it's also light, tasty, and healthy. Get to know your fishmonger, who'll prepare it for you so that it's ready to cook. Fish doesn't need elaborate techniques or sauces; it's delicious served simply. When shopping, look for fresh-smelling fish with bright eyes and a firm body with shiny skin and clean gills. Purchase on the day, or the day before, you plan to serve. For parties we do not advise serving anything with bones or shells in it. We feel it is also important to mention the global issue of vastly declining fish stocks and seriously damaged ecosystems that have been raising concerns among seafood consumers and the fishing industry – ask your fishmonger to identify the best environmental choice in seafood.

SEAFOOD

Prawns: The strongest advice we can give you about prawns is to BUY BIG! Small prawns for a glamorous party will look mean, so get the king size. Look for prawns in the shell that have no black spots, and always make sure you smell for freshness. Oriental supermarkets are a great place to buy frozen prawns, as they import excellent quality for a fair price. When preparing, peel off the shells, leave the tail and butterfly both sides, removing the veins. Prawns should not marinate for longer than 1 hour. They are best barbecued on skewers, char-grilled or pan-fried, and take just a few minutes to cook, so remove them from the heat as soon as they turn opaque.

Scallops: These little treasures are sweet, tender and terribly glamorous. If cost is not a consideration, scallops are impressive and easy to prepare. The smaller size are called 'queen' and work well as a canapé. For starters and main courses, use the large 'king scallop'. With their delicate flavour, scallops are beautiful with piquant sauces such as salsa verde (see page 87) or sweet chilli sauce. Do not remove the delicious pink coral – it is the tastiest part. Slice off the small white muscle found on the side of each scallop. Good scallops, if purchased really fresh, will keep in the fridge for 2 days before preparing. Searing and char-grilling are the best methods of cooking scallops. They only need 30 seconds to 1 minute for each side, otherwise they will overcook and shrink, losing their precious juices. For large parties, you can prepare scallops ahead. Briefly sear them on both sides, in a hot pan, then immediately cool and chill. Then, just before serving, roast them in a hot oven for about 4 minutes.

Crab: For most *Diva* recipes, buying crabs already dressed is recommended. If you do buy fresh whole ones, look for crabs that are heavy with the claws drawn tightly into the body. Use a hammer to break the body and crackers to open the legs. Discard the back part with the legs and any dubious looking pieces. We

only like using the white meat to cook with. The brown meat is stronger and not suitable for most prepared dishes. Crab is best known for its star role in crab cakes. Breadcrumbs and other ingredients can make a little meat go a long way. It is also beautiful in Thai salads, tarts, pastas and canapés.

SMOKED FISH

Smoked Salmon: Top-quality smoked salmon is readily available in vacuum-sealed packs. We like to use it for sophisticated canapés, served on toast cut into stars, mini blinis, cucumber cups or filo tartlets. It's also great in potato and summer pasta salads and pairs beautifully with capers, dill, crème fraîche, roasted peppers, and red onions.

Smoked Trout: With its bright pink colour, smoked trout looks dazzling and is used like smoked salmon. It contrasts well with pumpernickel, toasted and cut into shapes with horseradish. Crème fraîche, yogurt, red chillies, fresh coriander, and citrus sauces all marry well with it.

MEDITERRANEAN AND ROUND FISH

Monkfish: Monkfish is very popular due to its lack of bones and meaty texture. Because it's thick and sturdy, it can be poached, seared, roasted or barbecued, without falling apart. Look for monkfish that are firm, fresh-smelling, and that have the fine purple membrane removed – and buy on the day of preparation or the day before. Mediterranean ingredients partner best with it: olives, tomatoes, anchovies, capers, and saffron. Monkfish is wonderful in the classic soup – Bouillabaisse (see page 85).

Cod: Another member of the round fish family, cod was once relegated to only being prepared as fish and chips. As its scarcity continues, cod is slowly becoming an exclusive fish. Prized for its flaky white meat and light texture, it can be used with many flavours. It is delicious baked with potatoes, herbs and cream, and is equally superb steamed with Thai herbs, baked and drizzled with saffron aïoli or prepared with an exotic miso paste glaze. Look for thick, firm pieces of fish that have not been previously frozen.

Sea Bass: Its flaky white flesh is excellent poached, grilled, pan-fried, or baked, with a soft and delicate flavour. Look for firm, thick, fresh-smelling steaks or fillets. Works well with citrus vinaigrettes, herb sauces or garlic-roasted vegetables.

Halibut: Its firm white flesh may be an expensive delicacy, but it is sublime poached, braised or baked with white wine, cream, herbs, and lemon. Try to find firm, thick, steaks or fillets.

LARGE FISH

Tuna: There are many varieties of tuna: albacore, skipjack, yellowfin, and bluefin. Most are canned, except the exclusive bluefin – its prized red flesh is sold for sushi or fillet steaks. High quality fresh tuna is fabulous eaten raw, if consumed on the day of purchase, as sashimi, in a Latin ceviche or diced for Asian tartare. The texture is meat-like, so it stands up well to marinating and grilling. Strong ethnic flavours such as Moroccan, Japanese, Sicilian, Thai, or Mediterranean are best. It should be cooked rare, so sear it quickly on each side. It's wonderful in salads. To keep the flesh tight, buy a thin loin and roll in crushed peppercorns. Sear all over, then rest until cool. Wrap tightly in clingfilm and refrigerate overnight. Slice the next day.

Swordfish: Swordfish can be prepared similarly to fresh tuna. It's sold in steaks. In the markets of Palermo, you can see fishermen cutting off whole slices from a 1.2m (4ft) fish. Look for light pink steaks with little fat marbling. Swordfish absorbs marinades well. Strong flavours such as vinegars, charmoula, anchovies, lemon and garlic are wonderful partners. Lightly grill or pan-fry and serve with zesty salsas or vinaigrettes.

miso glazed cod

● Serves: 8 ● Preparation: 24 hours marinating and 10 minutes ● Cooking: 10 minutes

This is adapted from Nobu restaurant's signature dish. Of course they never give out their recipes, but through chatting to friendly waiters, a lot of tenacity, and careful testing, we think we've come pretty close.

8 x 175 g (6 oz) cod fillets (skin on)

the marinade

150 ml (5 fl oz) saké, Chinese rice wine or dry sherry

150 ml (5 fl oz) mirin

150 ml (5 fl oz) miso paste

2 tbsp light soy sauce

3 tbsp brown sugar

4 tbsp chopped spring onions to garnish

1 Place the fish in a shallow glass dish. Mix together the ingredients for the marinade, pour over the fish to coat thoroughly, then cover. Refrigerate for a minimum of 24 hours or up to 3 days (the fish is perfectly preserved with the salty miso).

2 Preheat a hot grill. Remove the fish from the marinade and place on a baking sheet, skin side down. Grill for 10 minutes, without turning, until cooked through. Serve immediately, sprinkled with the spring onions.

divados

 Do venture into a Japanese grocery shop to stock up on miso paste, mirin and saké.

 Try and allow 2–3 days for the fish to marinate. It makes a big difference to the flavour.

 Grill the fish just before your guests are ready to eat.

 Serve on its own with elegant lemon halves covered in yellow muslin, tied with ribbon – perfect for minimalists! Or serve with a selection of accompaniments, such as Tamarind-roasted Vegetables and Fragrant Coconut Rice (see pages 128 and 139).

divadon'ts

 Don't buy cod that has been previously frozen. Fresh cod is very important in this recipe.

monkfish, bacon, and dill pie with parmesan and spring onion mash

● Serves: 8   Preparation: 35 minutes   ● Cooking: 25 minutes

A classic favourite made slightly more up-market.

filling

55 g (2 oz) butter

1 onion, finely chopped

175 g (6 oz) rindless
streaky bacon, diced

500 g (1 lb 2 oz) monkfish fillet,
skinned and cut into chunks

2 leeks, thickly sliced.

25 g (1 oz) flour

400 ml (14 fl oz) milk

30 ml (1 fl oz) cream

4 tsp wholegrain mustard

25 g (1 oz) fresh dill, chopped

grated zest of ½ lemon

a pinch of nutmeg

salt and pepper

the topping

750 g (1 lb 10 oz) potatoes,
boiled and mashed

30 ml (1 fl oz) cream

25 g (1 oz) butter

4 spring onions, finely chopped

55 g (2 oz) parmesan cheese, grated

1 Preheat the oven to 180°C/350°F/Gas 4. Heat half the butter in a large non-stick frying pan. Add the onion and bacon, and sauté gently for 5 minutes. Add the fish and sauté until just sealed.

2 Blanch the leeks in boiling water for 5 minutes. Drain well.

3 Gently melt the remaining butter in a saucepan, stir in the flour and cook for 1 minute. Remove the pan from the heat and gradually add the milk and cream. Return to a low heat and bring to the boil, whisking continuously. Add mustard, dill, lemon zest, nutmeg, and seasoning.

4 Gently fold the fish mixture and leeks into the sauce, then spoon into a large ovenproof serving dish.

5 Mix the warm mashed potatoes with the cream, butter, spring onions, and Parmesan. Season to taste. Pile the mash on top of the fish and bake for 25 minutes until golden and crispy.

diva**dos**

 Any of your favourite fish, such as prawns, cod or smoked haddock, can be added to this versatile pie.

 This dish is excellent for winter parties as it can be prepared ahead and freezes well.

 Cut the monkfish into medium-sized chunks (no smaller), to keep them from breaking up.

 Start the evening off with Golden Shallot Pancakes with Tapenade (see page 10). For added glamour, make the pies in individual pots and garnish with chopped chives. Serve with a crispy salad of chicory, watercress and red onion.

seared tuna with couscous and sicilian vinaigrette

- Serves: 4 - Preparation: up to 1 hour marinating and 20 minutes - Cooking: 5 minutes

Sicilian cuisine is fascinating because of its strong roots in both North African and Italian ingredients. You won't find couscous in any other part of Italy. The capers and anchovies are the stars here, making everything burst with flavour.

450 ml (16 fl oz) couscous

a pinch of saffron powder or threads

125 ml (4 fl oz) boiling chicken stock

4 fresh tuna steaks

fresh coriander leaves to garnish

sicilian vinaigrette

2 tbsp capers, finely chopped

1 anchovy, rinsed and finely chopped

1 garlic clove, finely chopped

1 tsp crushed dried chillies

15 mint leaves, chopped

small handful of fresh coriander, chopped

a small handful of flat-leaf parsley, chopped

50 ml (2 fl oz) red wine vinegar (Cabernet Sauvignon)

125 ml (4 fl oz) extra virgin olive oil

salt and pepper

1 Place the couscous in a bowl. Add the saffron to the chicken stock, pour over the couscous and mix until coated. Spread it thinly up the sides of the bowl and leave to dry for 5 minutes.

2 Place the capers, anchovy, garlic, chillies and herbs in a screw-top jar. Add the vinegar and oil, screw on the lid tightly and shake well. Season to taste.

3 Pour ⅓ of the vinaigrette over the tuna steaks in a shallow dish. Leave to marinate for at least 5 minutes but ideally for 1 hour.

4 Just before serving, preheat a hot grill or barbecue. Crumble the couscous into fine grains then reheat in a steamer or microwave.

5 Grill or barbecue the tuna for 5 minutes, turning halfway through the cooking, until tender. Pile the couscous on a large plate, lay the tuna on top and garnish with coriander leaves. Pour the remaining vinaigrette over the fish and couscous, and serve immediately.

divados

 Look for tuna steaks that are bright red in colour with little fat. Swordfish steaks could also be used instead of tuna.

 Get ahead and prepare the couscous and vinaigrette the day before the event.

 Some lemon halves make an attractive garnish. Serve with Tuscan Panzanella Salad (see page 123).

divadon'ts

 Don't overcook tuna. It's best eaten medium-rare.

seared scallops and monkfish on curried red lentils with yogurt sauce

● Serves: 8　● Preparation: 30 minutes　● Cooking: 50 minutes

Red lentils cooked with fragrant spices and a refreshing yogurt sauce provide the perfect backdrop for delicate-tasting fish.

700 g (1 lb 9 oz) monkfish fillet, skinned

6 slices prosciutto

16 king scallops, trimmed

juice of ½ lemon

2 tbsp olive oil

salt and pepper

lentils

1 tbsp olive oil

1 onion, finely chopped

2 garlic cloves, chopped

2.5 cm (1 in) piece of fresh root ginger, peeled and grated

1 tsp ground cumin

1 tsp curry powder

225 g (8 oz) split red lentils

600 ml (1 pint) chicken stock

juice of ½ lemon

1 tbsp Greek yogurt

yogurt sauce

200 ml (7 fl oz) Greek yogurt

15 g (½ oz) fresh mint, chopped

1 green chilli, seeded and finely chopped

garnish

finely shredded spring onions

fresh coriander leaves

lemon wedges

1 Cut the monkfish into 16 even-sized chunks. Cut each slice of prosciutto into 3 and wrap a piece around each chunk of monkfish, including the little left over. Place scallops in a small bowl and toss with the lemon juice, 1 tbsp of the olive oil and seasoning.

2 To prepare the lentils, heat the olive oil in a large pan, add the onion, garlic, ginger, cumin, and curry powder, and sauté gently, stirring, for 3–4 minutes. Add the lentils and stir to coat for 2 minutes.

3 Add the stock, bring to the boil, then reduce the heat, cover and simmer for 45 minutes or until the

lentils are soft. Add the lemon juice, yogurt, and seasoning.

4 For the sauce, mix the yogurt, mint and chilli in a serving bowl.

5 Heat the remaining olive oil in a large non-stick frying pan. In batches, sear the scallops and monkfish parcels for 5 minutes or until cooked through. Drain off any liquid that weeps from the fish. Keep the cooked fish warm in a low oven.

6 To serve, spoon the warm curried lentils onto a platter, pile the fish on top and garnish with spring onions, coriander leaves and lemon wedges. Serve with the yogurt sauce.

diva**dos**

 We used scallops and monkfish, but you could use cod fillet and prawns or chunks of chicken breast tossed with crushed garlic, lemon juice and olive oil.

 The spiced lentils can be made a day ahead, then reheated over a low heat. A little extra chicken stock/water may be needed. The fish can be prepared for cooking the day before and kept covered in the fridge.

 To avoid over-cooking the fish in a last minute rush, sear it in a hot pan earlier in the day. Then place on a roasting tray and chill. Just before serving, roast the fish in a hot oven for 5–8 minutes.

 Start the evening off with Indian Pakoras (see page 12) and serve with a light green salad. Scoop up the sauce with our Cumin Flatbread (see page 163).

grilled swordfish with rosemary, tomato, and caramelized onions

● Serves: 8   ● Preparation: 1 hour marinating and 10 minutes   ● cooking: 1 hour

This recipe was inspired by a recipe from Tra Vigne, a restaurant in California's Napa Valley. It's quite Sicilian with its flavours of lemon zest, caramelized onions and sweet tomatoes and makes a lovely main course.

8 swordfish fillets, about 150 g (5½ oz) each

marinade

juice of 2 lemons

zest of 2 lemons

4 tbsp olive oil

1 tbsp chopped rosemary

salt and pepper

sauce

5 tbsp olive oil

5 onions, thinly sliced

2 tbsp chopped rosemary leaves

3 x 400 g cans peeled plum tomatoes

4 tbsp red wine vinegar

40 g (1½ oz) raisins, chopped

grated zest of 2 lemons

juice of 1 lemon

2 tbsp sugar

4 tbsp chopped flat-leaf parsley to garnish

1 Combine the ingredients for the marinade in a shallow dish. Add the fish and leave for at least 1 hour, covered and chilled.

2 To make the sauce, heat the olive oil in a saucepan and add the onions with the rosemary and seasoning. Cook gently for 20 minutes, stirring occasionally, until the onions start to caramelise.

3 When the onions are golden, add the tomatoes, vinegar, raisins, lemon zest, lemon juice, and sugar. Cook for 30 minutes or until the mixture is thick. Check seasoning.

4 Preheat a hot grill. Remove the fish from the marinade and cook or about 3 minutes on each side, depending on the thickness of the steaks – they may take a little longer.

5 To serve, pour the warm sauce into a large, deep platter, place the fish on top and scatter over the chopped parsley.

diva**dos**

 Do splash out at the fishmongers for the swordfish or other firm-fleshed fish, like sea bass or halibut. It's also worth spending a little more on good quality canned tomatoes for this dish.

 You can make the sauce the day before. Keep it chilled.

 Start your meal with Marinated Fig, Glazed Shallot and Prosciutto Salad or Tuscan Panzanella Salad (see pages 125 and 123). Follow with the fish.

diva**don'ts**

 Don't cook the fish until your guests are ready to eat.

diva**veggies**

tomato bruschetta with asparagus, gorgonzola, and basil salad

● Serves: 8 regular servings or 6 greedy ones   ● Preparation: 25 minutes

Our friend Rita lives in California and she is a regular shopper at the weekly farmers' market. She says that the ingredients are so superb that she now only arranges food instead of cooking it! This dish is not far off that concept and does require outstanding tomatoes.

topping

40 thin asparagus spears

1 tsp bicarbonate of soda

500 g (1 lb 2 oz) cherry tomatoes (preferably pomodorino)

2 garlic cloves, finely chopped

4 shallots, finely chopped

4 tbsp extra virgin olive oil

juice of 2 lemons

grated zest of 1 lemon

1 large bunch of basil, thinly sliced

salt and pepper

225 g (8 oz) Gorgonzola or dolcelatte cheese, crumbled

basil leaves to garnish

toasts

8 large slices of sourdough or French country bread, sliced at an angle

6 tbsp extra virgin olive oil

1 whole garlic clove, peeled

1 Trim the tough stalks from the asparagus, saving only the tender part of the stalks and the tips. Bring a large pan of lightly salted water to the boil. Add the bicarbonate of soda, then drop in the asparagus and blanch for 1 minute. Drain and immediately refresh in cold iced water to preserve the bright green colour – otherwise asparagus can turn an unappealing grey colour.

2 Slice the cherry tomatoes in half and mix together with the garlic, shallots, olive oil, lemon juice and zest, basil, and salt and pepper.

3 Preheat the oven to 200°C/ 400°F/Gas 6. Brush the bread with the olive oil and toast in the oven for about 4 minutes. Rub each bruschetta with the raw garlic clove. (If preferred, the toasts can be made under a hot grill.)

4 Drain the asparagus and pat dry with kitchen paper. Place 5 asparagus spears on each slice of bread. Pour over the tomato mixture over, dividing it equally between the bruschetta, and scatter the crumbled cheese over the top. Serve immediately, garnished with basil leaves.

diva**dos**

Buy the tomatoes a few days early and allow them to ripen in a bowl at room temperature. Please don't ever refrigerate tomatoes as it damages their flavour. Sourdough bread has a chewy texture that's perfect for bruschetta; a white country bread would also be fine.

Serve with any of the Diva tarts or barbecue dishes for a perfect summer party.

diva**don'ts**

Do not assemble the bruschetta until just before serving.

polenta-crusted aubergines with roasted tomatoes, buffalo mozzarella, and salsa verde dressing

- Serves: 8 • Preparation: 30 minutes salting and draining aubergines and 15 minutes
- Cooking: 1 hour

Let's face it, what doesn't taste good fried and served with salsa verde? Here, aubergines are made extra crispy with a coating of polenta, then served with roasted plum tomatoes, creamy mozzarella, and the wonderful herb sauce.

6 ripe plum tomatoes, halved

2 tbsp extra virgin olive oil

1 tbsp balsamic vinegar

salt and pepper

2 large aubergines, sliced into
1 cm (½ in) rounds

3 medium eggs

250 g (9 oz) polenta or fine cornmeal

850 ml (1½ pints) sunflower oil
for frying

2 buffalo mozzarella cheeses, each
torn into 6 pieces

salsa verde dressing

25 g (1 oz) flat-leaf parsley

25 g (1 oz) basil

1 tbsp capers, drained and washed

2 garlic cloves, peeled

1 tbsp red wine vinegar

125 ml (4 fl oz) extra virgin olive oil

1 Preheat the oven to 150°C/ 300°F/Gas 2. Lay the tomatoes on a baking tray, drizzle with olive oil and balsamic vinegar and season with salt and pepper. Roast for 1 hour.

2 Lay the aubergines on a large tray, sprinkle with salt and leave for 30 minutes. Whisk the eggs together in one bowl and place the polenta in another.

3 Heat the sunflower oil in a deep, heavy-based saucepan. Wipe the juices from the aubergines, drying at the same time with kitchen paper. Dip the aubergine slices first in the egg, then in the polenta, coating

thoroughly. Carefully fry in the hot oil, in small batches, until crisp and golden. Drain on kitchen paper.

4 Place all the ingredients for the salsa verde dressing in a food processor and puree until smooth. Season to taste.

5 To serve, arrange the hot aubergine slices around the edge of a large platter or individual serving plates. Place the roasted tomatoes in the centre, and scatter the mozzarella pieces over the top. Spoon the salsa verde over or pass separately in a bowl.

divados

 Salsa verde can be made with other green herbs such as coriander or mint.

 The salsa verde can be made a day ahead and kept covered and chilled. The tomatoes can also be roasted a day ahead.

 Do dry the aubergines well after rinsing. The slices can be coated with egg and polenta 30 minutes before frying. Once fried, they can be kept warm for 30 minutes.

 Serve as a starter or with Brochettes of Lemon Chicken, Sage and Croutons with Red Pepper Aïoli or Slow-roasted Tuscan Pork with Fennel (see pages 73 and 57).

roasted winter vegetables in a fragrant coconut sauce

● Serves: 8   ● Preparation: 30 minutes   ● Cooking: about 35 minutes

A colourful selection of root vegetables are roasted until sweet, then finished off with a delicately spiced coconut sauce. This is delicious with steamed basmati rice and a piquant chutney for a vegetarian main dish.

vegetables

700 g (1 lb 9 oz) sweet potatoes, peeled and cut into 2.5 cm (1 in) cubes

1 aubergine, cut into 2.5 cm (1 in) cubes

3 red onions, quartered

2 red peppers, seeded and cut into 2.5 cm (1 in) pieces

16 fresh baby corn

85 ml (3 fl oz) extra virgin olive oil

salt and pepper

coconut sauce

5 tbsp sunflower oil

2 large onions, finely chopped

10 garlic cloves, finely chopped

2 x 5 cm (2 in) pieces of fresh root ginger, peeled and grated

2 tbsp ground coriander

2 tbsp ground cumin

1 tsp salt

2 tsp turmeric

4 plum tomatoes, skinned and diced

2 x 400 g cans coconut milk

450 ml (16 fl oz) vegetable or chicken stock

15 g (½ oz) fresh coriander, chopped

20 mint leaves, chopped

1 Preheat the oven to 200°C/ 400°F/Gas 6. Place all the vegetables in a large roasting tray, and then drizzle over the olive oil and season with salt and pepper. Roast in the preheated oven for 20-30 minutes until the vegetables are golden. Remove from the oven and set aside.

2 Meanwhile, for the sauce, heat oil in a large saucepan, add the onions and sauté for 5 minutes,

then add the garlic and ginger. Cook for 3 minutes, stirring frequently, then add the spices and cook, stirring for 2 minutes.

3 Add the tomatoes, coconut milk, and stock, and simmer for 15 minutes.

4 Add the roasted vegetables to the sauce and then simmer for 5 minutes. Just before serving, add the chopped coriander and mint.

diva**dos**

 You can complete this dish totally up to 2 days ahead, then keep chilled until required.

 To reheat, warm gently in a covered pan or in a covered dish in a moderate oven. Do not stir too much, as you don't want to break up the vegetables.

 Serve with Fragrant Coconut Rice (see page 139) and a delicious tomato or mango chutney.

smoky black bean tacos with cherry tomato salsa

● Serves: 8   ● Preparation: 30 minutes plus overnight soaking   ● Cooking: 1 hour

This delectable black bean puree can be used as a dip or filling or made into bean cakes. If we were vegetarians, this is what we would live on! Cider vinegar, cumin and honey are the big flavours that give the beans a huge boost. Mix up some margaritas or sangria and have a fiesta.

500 g (1 lb 2 oz) dried black beans, soaked overnight

6 tbsp extra virgin olive oil

2 onions, chopped

2 red peppers, chopped

2 chipotle chillies in adobo sauce, or 2 dried chipotles, rehydrated in water (stemmed and seeded)

8 garlic cloves, chopped

2 tsp sea salt

150 ml (5 fl oz) cider vinegar

125 ml (4 fl oz) honey

2 tsp chilli powder

2 tsp ground cumin

16 corn tortillas

600 ml (1 pint) corn oil, for frying

the salsa

500 g (1 lb 2 oz) cherry tomatoes, halved

1 red onion, chopped

1 small bunch of fresh coriander, chopped

juice of 2 limes

salt and pepper

crème fraîche or soured cream to serve

1 Drain the soaked beans. Cover with fresh water in a medium saucepan, bring to the boil and simmer for 1 hour or until they are just tender.

2 Heat the olive oil in sauté pan. Add the onions, peppers, chillies, garlic, and salt. Sauté for 5 minutes, then add the beans. Stir in the vinegar, honey, chilli powder, and cumin. Simmer over a low heat for about 5 minutes, stirring occasionally.

3 Puree the beans in a food processor. Taste and adjust the seasoning. Scrape the mixture back into the sauté pan.

4 Heat the corn oil in a saucepan or deep-fat fryer. Place one tortilla at a time into the oil using a pair of tongs. Bend the tortilla slightly in half, so that it forms a taco shell. Be careful not to fold it too tight or it will be difficult to get the filling in. Fry for 1 minute until crispy, then drain on kitchen paper. Repeat until all the tortillas are deep-fried.

5 Mix together all the ingredients for the salsa.

6 To serve, spoon the warm beans into the taco shells and let guests help themselves to salsa and crème fraiche to spoon on top.

diva**dos**

Seek out corn tortillas from a Mexican speciality store, mail order company or an internet site. Once bought, you can freeze them for up to 4 months. If not available, use flour tortillas, sold in supermarkets. They will produce a more pastry-like texture when fried. Alternatively, flour tortillas can be used for wraps.

Do fry the tortillas up to 2 days ahead and keep in airtight container. The bean puree can be made up to 1 week ahead. Canned black beans require no soaking and can be used in place of dried.

The tortillas can also be fried flat to make tostados instead of tacos.

Serve with Tuna Ceviche or Grilled Prawns with Tamarind (see pages 32 and 82).

diva**don'ts**

Don't mix the salsa together until just before serving.

asian potato cakes with tomato sambal

● Makes: 12 cakes   ● Preparation: 50 minutes   ● Cooking: 30 minutes

We are mad about potato cakes! Deborah Madison of Greens restaurant in San Francisco inspired us years ago into making all kinds of them. This is adapted from one of her ideas.

potato cakes

750 g (1 lb 10 oz) potatoes, peeled and cut into large chunks

2 medium egg yolks

125 g (4½ oz) cheddar cheese, grated

4 spring onions, finely chopped.

25 g (1 oz) fresh coriander, chopped

3 green chillies, seeded and chopped

salt and pepper

125 g (4½ oz) sesame seeds

125 g (4½ oz) fresh breadcrumbs

sunflower oil for frying

lime wedges and fresh coriander sprigs to garnish

tomato sambal

1 quantity Tomato Sambal recipe (see page 22)

1 Cook the potatoes in lightly salted boiling water for about 10 minutes until soft and tender. Drain and leave to dry for 5 minutes.

2 Mash the potatoes with the egg yolks, cheese, spring onions, coriander, chillies and seasoning to taste. Mix well together.

3 Shape the mixture into 12 medium cakes using lightly floured hands. Mix the sesame seeds and breadcrumbs together. Roll the cakes firmly in the breadcrumb mixture, to coat all over. Chill until needed.

4 Heat 2.5 cm (1 in) of oil in a large, non-stick frying pan. Fry the cakes in batches for about 5 minutes, until browned all over. Keep warm in a medium oven.

5 Garnish the potato cakes with lime wedges and sprigs of coriander. Serve with the tomato sambal.

divados

 This recipe is so versatile – we often make a Mediterranean version, replacing the Cheddar with grated smoked mozzarella, chopped fresh basil in place of the coriander and 55 g (2 oz) chopped olives in place of the chillies. Omit the sesame seeds and double up the quantity of breadcrumbs. These are excellent served with Chunky Salsa Verde (see page 87).

 The potato cakes can be made a day ahead. Fry them one hour before serving and keep warm in a moderate oven.

 Ensure that the potatoes are drained really well, otherwise the mixture will be too wet.

 You can make these cakes smaller to serve as canapés (makes 24) or top the larger ones with crème fraîche, smoked trout pieces and little lime wedges to squeeze over.

divadon'ts

 Do not use a food processor to mash the potatoes, as they will turn to a puree. Mash by hand or using an electric whisk.

couscous with roasted sweet potato and harissa dressing

- Serves: 8   ● Preparation: 30 minutes soaking for the couscous and 15 minutes
- cooking: 40 minutes

Harissa is a treasure ingredient brought to us from North Africa. It's a piquant chilli paste that's used in everything from salads to grilled fish and meats. We've used it to spice up couscous with roasted vegetables and a lemony vinaigrette. Cool, minty yogurt is drizzled over for a delicious salad or vegetarian main dish.

couscous

300 g (10½ oz) couscous

250 ml (9 fl oz) vegetable stock

700 g (1 lb 9 oz) sweet potatoes, peeled and cut into chunks

4 red onions, cut into large chunks

3 red peppers, seeded and cut into large pieces

4 tbsp extra virgin olive oil

2 tbsp balsamic vinegar

1 x 400 g can chickpeas, drained

salt and pepper

dressing

150 ml (5 fl oz) extra virgin olive oil

150 ml (5 fl oz) lemon juice

grated zest of 1 lemon

2 tsp harissa paste

1 garlic clove, crushed

4 spring onions, finely chopped

handful of chopped mint, fresh coriander and parsley

the yogurt sauce

400 g (14 oz) plain greek yogurt

85 ml (3 fl oz) extra virgin olive oil

50 ml (2 fl oz) lemon juice

½ tsp ground cumin

handful of chopped mint, fresh coriander and parsley

1 Pour the boiling stock over the couscous in a bowl and leave to stand for 30 minutes. Preheat the oven to 200°C/400°F/Gas 6.

2 Arrange the sweet potatoes, onions and peppers in a roasting tin and drizzle with olive oil and vinegar. Roast for 40 minutes. Check after about 30 minutes, as you may need to remove the onions and peppers before the sweet potatoes, if they are already cooked. Leave to cool.

3 Mix all the dressing ingredients in a jar and set aside.

4 Mix together all the ingredients for the yogurt sauce. Chill until needed.

5 Break the couscous up with your fingers so that there are no lumps. Toss with the chickpeas and half of the dressing. Spread onto a large serving platter.

6 Mix the roasted vegetables with the remaining dressing and pile on top of the couscous. Serve the yogurt sauce separately.

diva**dos**

 You'll find harissa in the speciality or spice sections of most supermarkets. Remember to refrigerate it once opened.

 You can make the dressing and yogurt sauce the day before, omitting the herbs until shortly before serving. If making double the quantity of couscous, you'll need twice as much dressing.

 Serve with Spicy Prawns with Tomato Jam or Salad Mezze Plate (see pages 27 and 122). Or you can omit making the yogurt sauce and serve the couscous with our Lamb Fillet with Roasted Garlic, Coriander and Yogurt Sauce (see page 56).

diva**don'ts**

 Don't roast the vegetables more than 4 hours ahead, or they will lose their attractive appearance.

grilled red peppers stuffed with herbed ricotta and black olive vinaigrette

- Serves: 8 ● Preparation: 2 hours chilling and 50 minutes ● Cooking: 15 minutes

Stunning peppers packed with a creamy soft cheese, flavoured with sweet basil and sharp lemon, then topped off with a vinaigrette dressing, studded with black olives. Sensational!

8 red peppers

filling

250 g (9 oz) ricotta cheese

250 g (9 oz) cream cheese

1 tbsp extra virgin olive oil

grated zest of 1 lemon

85 g (3 oz) fresh basil, chopped

salt and pepper

the vinaigrette

6 tbsp extra virgin olive oil

2 tbsp balsamic vinegar

juice of ½ lemon

55 g (2 oz) pitted black olives, finely chopped

2 garlic cloves, finely chopped

1 tsp runny honey

2 tbsp chopped basil

a selection of mixed baby leaves to serve

basil leaves to garnish

1 Preheat a hot grill. Place the whole peppers under the heat and grill them all over, using tongs to turn, until the skins are nicely charred. Remove and place in a plastic bag to cool.

2 Carefully peel away and discard the skins from the peppers, trying not to tear the flesh. Chill until needed.

3 Mix together the filling ingredients, either by hand or in a food processor. Add salt and pepper to taste then cover and chill for at least 1 hour.

4 Place the vinaigrette ingredients in a screw-top jar and shake well.

5 To fill the peppers, carefully cut them open lengthways, down one side only, and remove the seeds and membranes. Lay the peppers flat and pat dry inside with kitchen paper. Spoon the ricotta mixture into the centre, dividing it evenly, then neatly roll up. Chill until ready to serve.

6 To serve, scatter the leaves on to a large serving plate or individual ones, place the peppers on top and drizzle the vinaigrette over and around. Garnish with basil leaves.

diva**dos**

 Any colour pepper will work. We love red and don't recommend green, but a mixture of colours would be festive. If liked, you could add some freshly grated Parmesan to the ricotta filling.

 The peppers can be grilled and skinned and the filling made a day ahead, then covered and kept in the fridge. The peppers can be stuffed 4 hours before serving and chilled. Drizzle over the vinaigrette at the last minute.

diva**don'ts**

 We don't advise roasting the peppers. Grilling keeps the flesh of the peppers firm.

babaganoush salad with goat's cheese and crispy pitta bread

● Serves: 8 ● Preparation: 25 minutes ● Cooking: about 1 hour

A classic salad from the Middle East is combined with goat's cheese to create a powerhouse of flavours. Eat it with our Cumin Flatbread or Diva Breadsticks for a delicious meal.

babaganoush

3 aubergines

2 garlic cloves

juice of 1 lemon

85 g (3 oz) tahini (sesame) paste

2 tbsp extra virgin olive oil

15 g (½ oz) fresh mint

salt and pepper

the crispy pitta bread

1 pkt of 8 white pittas

5 tbsp extra virgin olive oil

the salad

3 red peppers, halved

2 romaine or cos lettuce

4 plum tomatoes, quartered or 8 cherry tomatoes, halved

2 red onions, thinly sliced

500 g (1 lb 2 oz) goat's cheese log, crumbled or sliced

125 ml (4 fl oz) extra virgin olive oil, plus a little extra if grilling cheese

juice of 1 lemon

1 tsp runny honey

1 Preheat the oven to 190°C/ 375°F/Gas 5. Place the aubergines on a baking tray, prick several times and roast in the preheated oven for 30–40 minutes until blackened and soft. Remove and allow to cool

2 Slice the core end off the aubergines and peel away and discard the skins. Place the aubergine flesh in a food processor with the remaining babaganoush ingredients. Blend to a puree. Taste for seasoning.

3 Preheat a hot grill. Place the peppers, skin side uppermost, under the heat and grill until the skins have blackened. Remove and place in a plastic bag to cool. When cool, peel off the skins and discard, and cut the peppers into thick strips.

4 Cut the pitta breads into large chunks and toss with the olive oil, salt and pepper in a large bowl. Spread

on a baking sheet and bake at the same temperature for 10 minutes or until crisp.

5 To assemble the salad, take a large platter and arrange the lettuce leaves. Top with the tomatoes, onions and peppers, and then pile up the babaganoush in the centre. You can then either scatter the crumbled goat's cheese over the top or cut the cheese into thick slices and warm it under the grill.

6 To grill the cheese, place the slices on a baking tray, drizzle with a little olive oil and sprinkle with pepper. Grill for a few minutes until the cheese starts to brown and bubble. Arrange on top of the salad.

7 Whisk together the olive oil, lemon juice, honey and seasoning, and spoon the vinaigrette over the leaves. Serve the crispy pitta bread in a basket.

diva**dos**

 Feta could be used instead of goat's cheese.

 The crispy pitta can be made one day ahead and stored in an airtight container.

 The aubergines can be roasted over a barbecue, turning regularly. This adds a lovely smoky flavour.

 Don't bother with cutlery – this is so divine you can just scoop it up with the pitta and crispy lettuce.

gratin of balsamic wild mushrooms

● Serves: 8 ● Preparation: 15 minutes ● Cooking: 15 minutes

Wild mushrooms in a rich and creamy balsamic sauce, covered with a crunchy topping of breadcrumbs, Parmesan and fresh herbs.

mushroom mixture

4 tbsp extra virgin olive oil

225 g (8 oz) pied de mouton (hedgehog) mushrooms, chopped

350 g (12 oz) baby chestnut mushrooms, halved

125 g (4½ oz) fresh shiitake mushrooms, stemmed and quartered

4 shallots, finely chopped

4 garlic cloves, finely chopped

salt and pepper

50 ml (2 fl oz) balsamic vinegar

150 ml (5 fl oz) dry white wine

200 ml (7 fl oz) crème fraîche

topping

40 g (1½ oz) fresh white breadcrumbs

40 g (1½ oz) Parmesan cheese, finely grated

25 g (1 oz) Provolone or Gruyère cheese, finely grated

1 tbsp chopped thyme

1 tbsp chopped basil

3 tbsp chopped parsley

1 To prepare the topping, mix together all the ingredients in a bowl, season with salt and pepper and set aside.

2 For the mushroom mixture, heat the olive oil in a large saucepan on a medium-high heat. Add the pied de mouton and chestnut mushrooms, and gently saute for 3 minutes. Add the shiitake mushrooms, shallots, garlic and salt and pepper, and sauté for a further 3 minutes. Add the balsamic vinegar and cook for a few minutes until reduced by half.

3 Remove the mushrooms with a slotted spoon and place in a bowl. Reduce the heat and add the wine and crème fraîche to the juices in the pan. Heat gently, without allowing the sauce to boil, for about 5 minutes until thickened and reduced. Taste for seasoning and return the mushrooms to the sauce.

4 Preheat a hot grill. Pour the mushrooms into an ovenproof dish or individual ramekins and sprinkle the breadcrumb mixture over the top. Grill for 5 minutes or till crispy and golden.

diva**dos**

 Pied de Mouton are particularly good mushrooms to use because with their meaty texture they don't go soft quickly. However, any wild mushrooms can be substituted, such as girolles, chanterelles or field mushrooms. If you're feeling dangerous, use a bit of black truffle shaved over the top. Make this dish in autumn or winter, when wild mushrooms are in season.

 The mushroom mixture and topping can both be prepared a day ahead, then chilled. Bring to room temperature before baking.

 Grill the mushrooms just before serving to guests. Serve with a salad of radicchio, endive and rocket tossed with Classic Vinaigrette (see page 118).

goat's cheese baked in a spicy tomato sauce with garlic crostini

● Serves: 8   ● Preparation: 15-20 minutes   ● Cooking: about 1 hour

Creamy goat's cheese is baked with an intensely-flavoured, roasted tomato sauce. Garlicky crostini are used to scoop up delicious mouthfuls.

tomato sauce

1 kg (2¼ lb) ripe plum tomatoes, halved

4 tbsp extra virgin olive oil

2 tbsp balsamic vinegar

3 tbsp runny honey

4 garlic cloves, finely chopped

2 tsp dried crushed chillies

5–6 thyme sprigs

3 tbsp tomato puree

salt and pepper

crostini

1 large French stick, cut into 16 thick slices

50 ml (2 fl oz) extra virgin olive oil

1 whole garlic clove, peeled

250 g (9 oz) fresh goat's cheese log, with rind on

1 Preheat the oven to 200°C/ 400°F/Gas 6. Place the tomato halves in a shallow baking tray. Drizzle with the olive oil, balsamic vinegar and honey, then scatter over the garlic, chillies, half the thyme and seasoning. Bake for 30 minutes.

2 Place the roasted tomatoes in a food processor and blend. Add the tomato puree, then taste and add more honey if needed and salt and pepper to taste.

3 Preheat a hot grill. To make the crostini, brush each slice of bread with olive oil, then grill until golden and crispy. Rub the clove of garlic over each slice.

4 Place the tomato sauce in a medium-sized, ovenproof baking dish or 8 individual ramekins. Slice the goat's cheese into rounds and place on top of the sauce. Drizzle a little olive oil over, strip the leaves from the remaining thyme sprigs and sprinkle over the top with some black pepper.

5 Bake at 200°C/400°F/Gas 6 for 10–15 minutes until the cheese turns brown on top and the sauce is warm. To serve, place the dish in the centre of a large plate and arrange the garlic crostini around the edge.

divados

 The tomato sauce can be made well ahead and frozen, or make several days before and chill. Make the crostini up to 2 days before and store in an airtight container.

 Bake the dish with the goat's cheese topping just before serving.

 Serve as a starter before Spiedini of Scallops with Chunky Salsa Verde (see page 87) or simply with Diva Breadsticks (see page 158) and a spinach, radicchio and crouton salad with a gusty vinaigrette.

divadon'ts

 Don't use tomatoes that aren't ripened enough. Buy them at least 4 days before using.

divasalads

char-grilled mediterranean chicken salad with roasted garlic and basil dressing

- Serves: 8   • Preparation: 30 minutes   • Cooking: 1 hour

Invented for sunny days, this perfectly balanced salad, with its vibrantly green, gusty dressing, is the Mediterranean at its best.

8 boneless chicken breasts, skinned

juice of 1 lemon

250 g (9 oz) French beans, trimmed

3 red peppers, halved and seeded

1 red onion, thinly sliced

85 g (3 oz) sun-dried tomatoes, sliced

1 x 400 g can artichokes hearts, drained and quartered

25 g (1 oz) pitted black olives, halved

125 g (4½ oz) baby salad leaves to serve

basil leaves to garnish

roasted garlic and basil dressing

3 garlic bulbs

250 ml (9 fl oz) extra virgin olive oil

1½ tsp Dijon mustard

125 g (4½ oz) fresh basil

4 tbsp red wine vinegar

1 tsp runny honey

salt and pepper

1 Preheat the oven to 190°C/ 375°F/Gas 5. For the dressing, place the garlic bulbs on a baking sheet, drizzle with a little of the olive oil, then wrap tightly in foil and roast in the preheated oven for 45 minutes until soft. Remove foil and cool a liitle.

2 Cut the garlic bulbs in half and squeeze out the pulp. Place the pulp in a food processor with all the dressing ingredients except the olive oil. With the motor running, slowly drizzle in the oil to make a thick green dressing. Season to taste.

3 Heat a heavy griddle pan or char-grill plate and sear the chicken breasts on both sides for 5 minutes until cooked through. Remove from the heat, pour over the lemon juice and set aside.

4 Blanch the beans in salted boiling water for 3 minutes. Drain and refresh under cold water.

5 Preheat a hot grill. Lay the peppers, skin side up, under the heat and grill for about 10 minutes until charred and blistered. Remove and place in a plastic bag to cool. Skin the peppers and slice each half into quarters.

6 Mix all the vegetables together, except the salad leaves, and toss with half the dressing. Scatter the salad leaves on to a large platter and pile the vegetables on top. Slice the chicken on a slant and arrange on the salad, then spoon over the remaining dressing and garnish with basil leaves.

diva**dos**
Fresh artichokes or fresh tomatoes can be used if preferred. You could also add toasted pine nuts.

If making for a crowd, char-grill the chicken for 1 minute on each side, then roast for 10 minutes in a hot oven, sprinkled with lemon juice, olive oil and seasoning.

vietnamese minced chicken salad

● Serves: 8   ● Preparation: 15 minutes   ● Cooking: 5 minutes

This refreshing salad is a modern take on the classic Vietnamese pork 'larb' salad. We think that chicken breast is lighter, juicier and more attractive. It has all the classic flavours of sweet, salty, and sour that characterise south-east Asian food.

6 boneless chicken breasts, skinned and roughly chopped

3 tbsp groundnut oil

1 large red onion, chopped

3 tbsp grated fresh root ginger

3 small red chillies, seeded and chopped

40 g (1½ oz) fresh coriander, chopped

2 iceberg or 4 little gem lettuce, separated into leaves

fresh coriander leaves to garnish

dressing

50 ml (2 fl oz) fresh lime juice

124 ml (4 fl oz) fresh lemon juice

4 tbsp Thai fish sauce (nam pla)

2 tbsp caster sugar

salt to taste

1 Place the chicken breasts in a food processor and pulse until minced. Heat the oil in a wok or large frying pan until almost smoking. Cook the chicken for about 5 minutes until it turns white, breaking it up thoroughly with a large fork. Make sure you drain off any excess liquid that comes out of the chicken. Transfer to a bowl and then add the onion, ginger, chillies and chopped coriander. Toss well.

2 In a small bowl, combine the lime and lemon juices, fish sauce, sugar and 2 tbsp water. Toss the chicken with this dressing and season with salt to taste.

3 Pile the lettuce leaves, a couple on top of each other, making individual 'bowls'. Just before serving, spoon the chicken salad into the lettuce 'bowls' and sprinkle a few coriander leaves over the top.

diva**dos**

 Do mince fresh chicken breasts rather than buying ready-minced chicken.

 Serve as a canapé in cucumber cups, on baby gem lettuce leaves or in Wonton Cups (see page 31) or as part of an Oriental menu with Asian Potato Cakes, Roast Fillet of Beef and Prawn Dumplings in Fragrant Thai Broth (see pages 104, 66 and 88).

diva**don'ts**

 Don't make the chicken mixture more than 2 hours ahead, or the onion will dominate the flavour.

dressings and vinaigrettes

When it comes to dressings and vinaigrettes, a little goes a long way! Most of these ingredients are used sparingly and will last for ages in your store cupboard. Simply following recipes is difficult because everyone's palate is different. So pour your ingredients into a lidded jam jar, shake and taste!

OILS

Extra Virgin Olive Oil: For vinaigrettes and drizzling. When mixing vinaigrettes, start with ⅓ vinegar and ⅔ oil, then adapt to taste.

Olive Oil: For searing, marinades and lighter dressings. If you are heating foods, use olive oil.

Walnut Oil: Partner with fruit, nuts and cheese. Great winter oil.

Hazelnut Oil: Similar to walnut oil, but more powerful.

Sunflower Oil: For mayonnaise or mixed with extra virgin olive oil to give a lighter touch.

MUSTARDS

Dijon: Great emulsifier, and helps create a creamy, nutty flavour. Excellent for use in Mediterranean dressings. Make sure you use sparingly, as the flavour should not be dominant.

Whole Grain: Sharp flavour and texture. Good for potatoes, mayonnaises and meat salads.

VINEGARS

Cabernet Sauvignon: Gives dressings an intense red wine flavour; ideal for sharp vinaigrettes. A key ingredient for Greek salads.

Sherry: Strong, smoky and nutty aroma. Excellent when paired with walnut oil. Try on bitter lettuces, for example Belgian endive and radiccio, with some pancetta.

Red Wine: Is this the world's most versatile vinegar? Try adding ½ tsp of caster sugar to create a simple vinaigrette.

Balsamic: Sweet; complements the majority of Mediterranean foods. Excellent mixed with light soy sauce and ginger.

Rice Wine: For oriental dressings.

Cider: Workhorse for hearty fare; wonderful in potato salads.

Champagne: Elegant and light; good with peppery greens.

CITRUS

Lemon: The rind and juice are both key ingredients for agrodolce flavour, that wonderful sweet and sour taste.

Lime: Absolutely essential component of Asian vinaigrettes.

Orange: To add sweetness, mix it with lemon or lime.

FLAVOURS

Honey: A little honey goes a long way. It partners well with red wine vinegar, sherry vinegar, citrus juice and Asian salad vinaigrettes.

Pomegranate Molasses: The magic ingredient for Middle Eastern salads, particularly those containing green beans, aubergines, lamb, duck,

couscous and bulgar wheat. Mix, in place of vinegar, with oil, lemon juice and sugar to make a delicious dressing.

Soy Sauce: Asian essential. Use with balsamic vinegar and sunflower oil to make an oriental vinaigrette.

Fish Sauce: Southeast Asia's powerhouse ingredient; pair with sugar and lime.

DAIRY

Blue Cheese: A sublime partner for bitter chicory, endive or potatoes. To make a classic blue cheese dressing, crumble into crème fraiche with lemon, salt and pepper. Great on crunchy iceberg lettuce or a grilled steak.

Parmesan: Nutty, salty and creamy. Only buy the parmesan stamped 'parmigiano reggiano', as this means it is authentic and has been aged for two years.

Yogurt: A light and healthy option for Middle Eastern salads – although we favour Greek yogurt, which is the creamiest variety.

Crème Fraîche: Creamy partner for potatoes, ham or bacon in salads. Don't substitute the low-fat variety, as it lacks depth of flavour.

FRESH HERBS

Basil: Lovely in Mediterranean or Asian dressings.

Chives: Complement red wine or sherry vinegar dressings; great on salads with meat or potatoes.

Flat-leaf Parsley: Superior to the curly variety, this versatile herb is brilliant in all Mediterranean dressings.

Coriander: Used in Asian, Mexican and Mediterranean dressings, coriander is lovely in chilli-lime vinaigrettes.

Tarragon: The French variety has a better flavour than the Russian. Lovely accompaniment to potato salads.

Oregano: Use with tomatoes drizzled with olive oil and red wine vinegar.

SPICES

Cumin: Smoky-flavoured spice for Mexican or Middle Eastern dressings.

Coriander Seeds: Best crushed when used in dressings. Pairs well with yogurt dressings. A fresh supply is vital as flavour is lost over time.

Fennel Seeds: Best crushed or ground when used in dressings. Complements Mediterranean salads best.

Chilli: A little kick is a great addition, but use sparingly. Be aware that different varieties have different strengths; above all, take care not to mask the flavour of the food.

Sea Salt: We beg you not to use bleached table salt! Sea salt enhances and softens vegetables when used in cooking. Add salt at the beginning of cooking, not the end, or the dish will taste like you added salt.

Black Pepper: Freshly ground gives the best flavour and texture.

PIQUANT FLAVOURS

Olives: Only buy pitted, high-quality olives soaked in olive oil.

Capers: Try to buy salt-packed. Rinse and soak in warm water for 5 minutes in order to remove salt. When chopped to a rough paste, capers add a magical depth to vinaigrettes.

Anchovies: Buy the variety that comes in olive oil. People who swear they hate them will swoon over a dish in which they aren't visible. Rinse with cool water and chop to a fine paste.

Sun-blush tomatoes: These are only partially dried, leaving them intense yet still moist. Chop finely to create a gorgeous Mediterranean vinaigrette.

master recipes for vinaigrettes and mayonnaise

classic mayonnaise   Makes: 300 ml (10 fl oz)

2 tbsp white wine vinegar

2 egg yolks, at room temperature

1 tbsp Dijon mustard

1 tbsp soft brown sugar

½ tsp each of salt and pepper

250 ml (9 fl oz) sunflower oil

1 Combine all the ingredients, except for the oil, in a blender or food processor. Then, with the motor running, slowly drizzle in the oil until it is all incorporated.

2 This mayonnaise will keep for 4 days in the fridge.

variations
- Add 1 tsp saffron threads soaked in 2 tbsp hot water.
- Add 3–4 finely chopped garlic cloves for a garlic mayonnaise or aïoli.
- Add any chopped fresh herbs, such as tarragon, rosemary, basil, or coriander.

classic vinaigrette   Makes: 150 ml (5 fl oz)

1 shallot, finely chopped

1 tsp Dijon mustard

4 tbsp red wine vinegar (sherry, Cabernet Sauvignon or balsamic can also be used)

90 ml (3 fl oz) extra virgin olive oil

1 garlic clove, finely chopped

salt and pepper

1 Place all the ingredients in a screw-top jar and shake well together. Season to taste with salt and pepper.

2 This will keep for 1 week in the fridge. Bring to room temperature and shake well before using.

variations
- Add chopped capers.
- Or finely chopped hard-boiled egg
- Or finely chopped anchovies
- Or finely chopped fresh herbs, like basil or oregano.

classic oriental dressing   makes: 150 ml (5 fl oz)

2 tbsp rice wine vinegar

2 tbsp light soy sauce

2 tbsp fresh lime juice

1 tbsp groundnut oil

1 tbsp caster sugar

1 garlic clove, finely chopped

1 spring onion, finely chopped

a small bunch of fresh coriander, chopped

1 Place all ingredients in a screw-top jar and shake well together.

2 This will keep for 1 week in the fridge. Shake well before using.

variations
- Add grated fresh root ginger.
- Or chopped fresh herbs, such as Thai basil or mint leaves
- Or mirin in place of the rice wine vinegar
- Or about 1 tbsp Thai fish sauce
- Or grated lime zest.

soba noodle salad with roasted aubergine and soy-balsamic dressing

● Serves: 8 ● Preparation: 25 minutes ● Cooking: 35 minutes

So many noodle salads look tasty, but are dry and bland. This was inspired by a recipe in Deborah Madison's 'Greens' cookbook. It's one of the few Oriental noodle salads that has depth and taste.

750 g (1 lb 10 oz) aubergines (small if possible)

500 g (1 lb 2 oz) Japanese soba noodles

10 asparagus spears, cut diagonally into 2.5 cm (1 in) pieces

4 tbsp sesame seeds, toasted

fresh coriander leaves to garnish

soy-balsamic dressing

125 ml (4 fl oz) sesame oil

125 ml (4 fl oz) light soy sauce

6 tbsp balsamic vinegar

6 tbsp caster sugar

2 tbsp chilli pepper oil

2 garlic cloves, finely chopped

3 tbsp grated fresh root ginger

15 spring onions, finely sliced

a small handful of fresh coriander, finely chopped

1 Preheat the oven to 200°C/ 400°F/Gas mark 6. Prick the aubergines several times with a sharp knife, then bake for 25 minutes (longer if large) until soft. Remove, slice in half lengthways and leave to cool. Peel away and discard the skins. Roughly chop the flesh and leave to drain in a colander.

2 Mix together all the dressing ingredients. Dress the chopped aubergine with half the dressing and reserve the rest.

3 Cook the noodles in salted boiling water for about 5 minutes until al dente. Drain and rinse under cold water. Place in large bowl, pour over the remaining dressing and mix evenly, using your fingers.

4 Blanch the asparagus in a large pan of salted boiling water. Drain and refresh in cold water, drain again and pat dry with kitchen paper. Toss the asparagus with the noodles, aubergines and sesame seeds. Garnish with coriander leaves.

diva**dos**

 Chinese egg noodles can be used in place of soba noodles. Do seek out small aubergines – they are less bitter than the larger ones. If not available, use long, firm and shiny-skinned aubergines.

 Make the dressing the day before and the salad on the morning of the party.

 Serve with other refreshing dishes, such as Seared Thai Chicken with Tomato-Chilli Jam (see page 80).

thai green papaya salad with seared chilli prawns

● Serves: 8   ● Preparation: 1 hour marinating and 30 minutes   ● cooking: 2 minutes

This classic Thai salad normally includes tiny dried shrimp, but as these are not easily found or admired by all, we have jazzed it up with gloriously marinated and seared king prawns.

40 raw king prawns, peeled

marinade

1 tbsp chilli sauce

1 tsp runny honey

1 tsp grated fresh root ginger

juice and grated zest of 1 lime

1 tbsp extra virgin olive oil for searing

salad

1 large green papaya, peeled, seeded and grated into long strips

10 mange-tout, cut into juilienne

3 tomatoes, seeded and diced

2 garlic cloves, finely chopped

½ tsp dried red chilli flakes

25 g (1 oz) roasted peanuts, chopped

1 tbsp caster sugar

2 tbsp Thai fish sauce (nam pla)

2 tbsp fresh lime juice

fresh coriander sprigs to garnish

1 Mix together the chilli sauce, honey, ginger, lime juice and zest, pour over the prawns and leave to marinate for 1 hour.

2 Place the strips of papaya in a large bowl with the mange-tout, tomatoes, garlic and chilli flakes. Set aside.

3 Preheat a heavy griddle or frying pan, add the olive oil and sear the prawns for about 2 minutes until pink.

4 Add the peanuts, sugar, fish sauce and lime juice to the papaya mixture, taste and add a little more of any of the flavouring ingredients, if liked.

5 Pile the salad on to a large serving plate, place the seared prawns around the edge and garnish with coriander sprigs.

diva**dos**

 This salad can be made with seeded cucumber cut into thin strips in place of the papaya, although it's not quite the same, as cucumber is very watery. The salad also works well with scallops instead of prawns.

 The salad can be prepared a day ahead, but do not add the peanuts or dressing until 30 minutes before you are ready to serve.

 The prawns can be served hot or cold, or even mixed into the salad, once cold. Julienned red chilli or spring onion also makes an attractive garnish. Serve with Seared Thai Chicken or Grilled Indonesian Coconut Chicken (see pages 80 and 18).

salad mezze plate

● Serves: 8   ● Preparation: 1 ¼ hours   ● Cooking: 35 minutes

Mezze, like antipasti, is a flavourful selection of 'little' dishes. It's a great way to start a party and have everyone digging in and enjoying a colourful feast.

aubergine puree

2 large aubergines

3 tbsp extra virgin olive oil

125 g (4½ oz) Greek yogurt

grated zest and juice of ½ lemon

15 g (½ oz) mint, stalks removed

2 garlic cloves

½ tsp ground allspice

salt and pepper

chickpea salad

1 x 400 g can chickpeas, drained

2 red chillies, seeded and finely chopped

1 red onion, finely chopped

15 g (½ oz) fresh coriander, finely chopped

15 g (½ oz) mint, finely chopped

juice of ½ lemon

1 garlic clove, finely chopped

1 tbsp pomegranate molasses

4 tbsp extra virgin olive oil

1 tsp cumin seeds, toasted

salt and pepper

85 g (3 oz) feta cheese to garnish

fresh coriander leaves to garnish

aubergine puree

1 Preheat the oven to 190°C/ 375°F/Gas 5. Prick the aubergines several times with a fork, place on a roasting tray and roast for 35 minutes until blistered and softened. Remove and allow to cool. Cut off the stems, and peel away and discard the skins.

2 Place the aubergine pulp in a food processor with all the remaining ingredients. Puree until smooth. Cover and keep cool until needed.

chickpea salad

1 Place the chickpeas in a food processor and pulse until just crushed. Remove and place in a large bowl with the rest of the ingredients. Stir well and season to taste.

2 Garnish with the feta crumbled over and scatter with the coriander leaves.

diva**dos**

Serve with either our Cumin Flatbread or Pitta Breadsticks (see pages 163 and 11) or with other great Mediterranean dishes like Lamb Fillet with Roasted Garlic, Coriander and Yogurt or Pomegranate-marinated Lamb Cutlets with Coriander Tabbouleh (see pages 56 and 59).

grilled pepper salad

3 red and 3 orange peppers, quartered and seeded

1 tbsp harissa paste or chilli sauce

5 tbsp extra virgin olive oil

40 g (1½ oz) pitted black olives, chopped

55 g (2 oz) toasted pine nuts, chopped

15 g (½ oz) basil, thinly sliced

salt and pepper

1 Preheat a hot grill. Grill the peppers until the skins have blackened, then place in a plastic bag to cool.

2 Mix the harissa and olive oil together. Skin the peppers and cut the flesh into thick slices. Place in a bowl and add the harissa oil, olives, pine nuts, basil and seasoning.

tuscan panzanella salad

● Serves: 8   ● Preparation: 45 minutes   ● Cooking: 7 minutes

Panzenella is not often seen in restaurants outside of Tuscany. Lush cherry tomatoes, crunchy cucumber, capers and chewy bread create a myriad punchy flavours and textures. It's a wonderful salad for summer when the vegetables are at their peak.

1 large Italian ciabatta or sourdough loaf, sliced and cut into bite-sized chunks

300 g (10½ oz) cherry tomatoes, halved

3 celery stalks, sliced

3 red peppers, roasted, peeled and sliced into strips

10 Italian black olives, pitted and halved

3 tbsp capers, well-rinsed

1 large red onion, finely chopped

2 mini cucumbers (or 1 large cucumber, seeded), peeled and diced large

2 handfuls of basil, sliced

1 garlic clove, finely chopped

1 anchovy, rinsed and chopped

the dressing

125 ml (4 fl oz) extra virgin olive oil

125 ml (4 fl oz) red wine vinegar (Cabernet Sauvignon) or balsamic vinegar

salt and pepper

8 halved fresh anchovies to garnish (optional)

1 Preheat the oven to 200°C/ 400°F/Gas 6. Place the bread on a baking tray, drizzle with a little olive oil and sprinkle with seasoning. Bake for 7 minutes or until crispy. Remove and allow to cool.

2 Combine all the ingredients, except the dressing, in a large salad bowl.

3 When ready to serve, pour over the oil and vinegar, sprinkle with salt and pepper and garnish, if liked, with the fresh anchovies laid over the top.

diva**dos**

 Do use ripe cucumbers and tomatoes, as flavour is important in this salad. Plum or vine-ripened tomatoes, cut into chunks, can replace the cherry tomatoes. Fresh anchovies, from a deli, are pure white in colour and look and taste nothing like the canned variety.

 The croutons can be made a day ahead and stored in an airtight container. The vegetables should not be sliced more than 4 hours ahead, then not combined until ready to serve.

 Serve with other great Mediterranean dishes during the summer, like Slow-roasted Tuscan Pork, Lamb Fillet with Roasted Garlic, Coriander and Yogurt or Brochettes of Lemon Chicken (see pages 57, 56 and 73).

marinated fig, glazed shallot, and prosciutto salad with parmesan crisps

● Serves: 8   ● Preparation: 4 hours marinating and 30 minutes   ● Cooking: 50 minutes

Our passion for cooking with figs and creating new salads was how this stunning recipe was invented. The crunchy parmesan crisps and prosciutto are wonderful against the luscious figs.

8 fresh ripe figs, quartered

2 tbsp extra virgin olive oil

1 tbsp balsamic vinegar

16 small shallots, peeled

1 tsp golden caster sugar

85 g (3 oz) Parmesan cheese, freshly grated

8 slices of prosciutto

175 g (6 oz) rocket leaves or watercress to serve

the vinaigrette

1 tsp Dijon mustard

1 garlic clove, finely chopped

1 small red onion, finely chopped

2 tbsp balsamic vinegar

200 ml (7 fl oz) extra virgin olive oil

salt and pepper

1 Place the figs on a plate, sprinkle with half the olive oil and vinegar and leave to marinate for about 4 hours.

2 Preheat the oven to 180°C/ 350°F/Gas 4. Place the shallots in a roasting tin, drizzle with the remaining oil and vinegar, sprinkle with sugar and seasoning, then roast for 40 minutes, regularly shaking the pan. Remove and set aside. Increase the temperature to 190°C/375°F/Gas 5.

3 To make the Parmesan crisps, line 2 baking trays with greaseproof paper and sprinkle the Parmesan evenly into 2 x 20 cm (8 in) round circles. Bake for 3 minutes, until bubbling. Remove from the oven, cool for 1 minute, then slice each circle into 4 triangles.

Separate the triangles slightly on the paper, then return to the oven for another 3 minutes until golden. Remove and cool on a wire rack. Handle with care!

4 Lay the prosciutto directly on to a baking tray and roast at the same temperature for 5 minutes to crisp. Cool on kitchen paper.

5 Whisk together the vinaigrette ingredients. Season to taste.

6 To serve, pile the rocket leaves on individual plates and divide the figs and shallots among them. Place the prosciutto on top, spoon over the vinaigrette and garnish each serving with a Parmesan crisp.

diva**dos**

 Parma, serrano or Bayonne ham can also be used, or even crispy rashers of smoked streaky bacon. Add your favourite blue cheese to this salad for a delicious variation. Caramelised quartered red onions can replace the glazed shallots.

 The Parmesan crisps can be made a day ahead. Store in an airtight container. Make the vinaigrette several days ahead and keep in a screw-top jar. Roast the shallots one day ahead – do not chill.

 Parmesan crisps are so simple, but keep an eye on them as the cooking time may vary slightly for different ovens.

 Assemble no more than 20 minutes before serving. This makes an elegant starter before Spiedini of Scallops or Butterflied Leg of Lamb (see pages 87 and 64).

thai beef salad

● Serves: 8   ● Preparation: 1 hour marinating and 30 minutes   ● cooking: 20 minutes

This classic Thai dish has been very popular recently for a very good reason – it's so delicious! Healthy and bursting with flavour, we think it's the best combination we've ever tasted.

1 kg (2 lb 4 oz) lean beef fillet or sirloin steak

1 tbsp Thai fish sauce (nam pla)

2 tsp black peppercorns, crushed

20 leaves of cos or little gem lettuce

1 large red onion, thinly sliced

500 g (1 lb 2 oz) cherry or pomodorino tomatoes, halved

8 mini cucumbers, cut into julienne

2 large red chillies, seeded and cut into julienne

fresh coriander leaves to garnish

vinaigrette

125 ml (4 fl oz) fresh lime juice

2 tbsp Thai fish sauce (nam pla)

1 tsp light soy sauce

1 tsp sweet chilli sauce

2 tsp sugar

1 garlic clove, crushed

a handful of fresh coriander, chopped

handful of mint, chopped

1 lemongrass stalk, thinly sliced

1 Marinate the beef in the fish sauce and peppercorns for at least 1 hour or overnight, covered and chilled.

2 Place all the vinaigrette ingredients in a screw-top jar and shake together.

3 Preheat the oven to 200°C/ 400°F/Gas 6. Sear the beef on both sides in a hot frying pan until browned. Transfer to a roasting pan and roast for 15 minutes until just

medium-rare. Rest for 10 minutes, then thinly slice.

4 Line a platter with lettuce leaves. Place the onions, tomatoes, cucumbers, and chillies in a large bowl and toss with half the vinaigrette. Pile on top of the lettuce leaves.

5 Arrange the beef elegantly around the edge of the platter and spoon the remaining vinaigrette over the meat. Scatter coriander over the salad to garnish.

diva**dos**

 Look for fat juicy limes by giving them a good squeeze test at the shops.

 Prepare everything in the morning then dress just before serving.

 The beef can be served hot or cold in this salad.

 Serve with Seared Thai Chicken, Thai Green Papaya Salad or Asian Potato Cakes (see pages 80, 120 and 104) for a fabulous Asian feast.

greek chicken salad with caper and anchovy vinaigrette

● Serves: 8 regular servings or 6 greedy ones   ● Preparation: 25 minutes plus 1 hour or overnight marinating   ● Cooking: 10 minutes

Here we've combined creamy feta cheese, the ripest cucumbers, and tomatoes with grilled chicken and an anchovy-spiked dressing.

6 boneless chicken breasts, skinned

marinade

grated zest and juice of 2 lemons

5 tbsp extra virgin olive oil

1 tsp chopped oregano

salt and pepper

salad

300 g (10½ oz) cherry or pomodorino tomatoes, halved

1 large red onion, finely chopped

2 mini cucumbers (or 1 large cucumber, seeded), peeled and sliced

2 tbsp chopped fresh oregano (or 2 tsp dried)

250 g (9 oz) imported feta cheese, cut into 1 cm (½ in) cubes

caper and anchovy vinaigrette

2 anchovies in oil, well rinsed and finely chopped

20 small capers, rinsed and finely chopped

2 garlic cloves, finely chopped

150 ml (5 fl oz) red wine vinegar (Cabernet Sauvignon)

175 ml (6 fl oz) extra virgin olive oil

1 Combine the ingredients for the marinade and marinate the chicken for at least 1 hour or overnight.

2 Place all the vinaigrette ingredients in a screw-top jar, add seasoning and shake well.

3 Preheat a heavy griddle pan, char-grill plate or barbecue. Remove the chicken from the marinade and sear

for 5 minutes on each side until cooked through. Remove the chicken, cover and rest for 5 minutes, then carve into thin, diagonal slices.

4 Combine the tomatoes, onion, cucumber, chicken and oregano in a large bowl. Add the feta.

5 Just before serving, pour over the dressing and toss together.

diva**dos**

Buy creamy feta cheese imported from Greece or Lebanon. Domestic types can be too salty. Lebanese and Greek shops are also wonderful sources for mini cucumbers and yogurt. Use ripe cherry tomatoes – they are far less watery than larger ones. Cabernet Sauvignon vinegar has a unique cherry flavour, but if unavailable, use a good quality red wine vinegar.

Prepare the vegetables on the morning of the party. The chicken can be served warm or cold. If served cold, it can be cooked the day before, chilled and covered.

diva**extras**

tamarind-roasted vegetables

● Serves: 8 ● Preparation: 20 minutes ● Cooking: 45 minutes

Move over roast potatoes, there's a new side dish in town. Winter root vegetables, red peppers and baby corn are sweetened by roasting and then tossed in a spicy tamarind glaze. A perfect partner for Asian dishes or just eaten on its own with rice.

16 fresh baby corn

4 large sweet potatoes, peeled and cut into 1 cm (½ in) cubes

3 red, yellow or orange peppers, cut into 2.5 cm (1 in) pieces

3 red onions, quartered

4 baby beetroots, halved (or 2 large beetroots, quartered)

16 whole shallots, peeled

4 tbsp groundnut oil

tamarind glaze

125 ml (4 fl oz) bottled tamarind puree.

3 garlic cloves

2 tsp freshly grated ginger

2 lemongrass stalks, peeled of outer layers, top ⅓ removed and chopped

2 medium-sized red chillies, seeded and stems removed

10 mint leave

15 g (½ oz) fresh coriander (separate stems and leaves)

2 tbsp honey

1 tsp each of salt and pepper

1 First make the glaze. Place the tamarind, garlic, ginger, chopped lemongrass, chillies, mint, coriander stems, honey, and salt and pepper in a food processor. Blend to a puree and taste for seasoning. Add extra honey if liked.

2 Preheat the oven to 200°C/400°F/Gas 6. Place the vegetables on a large baking tray (or use 2 trays),

toss with the groundnut oil and season with salt and pepper. Bake for 30 minutes then remove from the oven.

3 Pour over the tamarind mixture, mix with the vegetables, then place back in the oven. Roast for a further 15 minutes until nicely glazed.

4 Garnish with the coriander leaves.

diva**dos**

 If liked, you can replace the sweet potatoes with butternut squash or pumpkin. You can make your own tamarind puree by soaking a chunk of tamarind pulp in warm water and sieving the liquid. Be sure to keep it refrigerated.

 The vegetables can be chopped the day before and the tamarind glaze made up to 2 days ahead.

 Serve these vegetables as a main course meal with Fragrant Coconut Rice (see page 139) or with any Asian dishes like Korean Barbecued Chicken (see page 71), as a perfect complement.

diva**don'ts**

 Do not overcrowd the baking trays with vegetables or they will produce too much steam and prevent the vegetables from crisping.

sweet potato and ginger mash

● Serves: 8 ● Preparation: 10 minutes ● Cooking: 25 minutes

We love sweet potatoes for their vibrant colour and sweet creamy taste. This is a stunning mash to serve with any Asian or Mediterranean dish.

1.1 kg (2 lb 8 oz) orange sweet potato, peeled and cut into large chunks

55 g (2 oz) butter

5 cm (2 in) piece of fresh root ginger, peeled and grated

2 tbsp olive oil

salt and pepper

chopped fresh coriander to garnish

1 Place the sweet potato chunks in a saucepan of lightly salted, cold water. Bring to the boil then reduce the heat, cover and simmer for 20 minutes until tender. Drain well in a colander.

2 While the potatoes are draining, melt the butter in the pan and add the grated ginger. Soften for 5 minutes, then return the potatoes to the pan. Add the olive oil and seasoning. Mash until soft.

3 Serve hot, scattered with lots of coriander.

diva**dos**

 We recommend using the most common sweet potato with orange/brown skin and bright orange flesh. Be careful not to buy the purple, white fleshed sweet potato – it has a poor colour and tastes far too sweet. You can also use butternut squash instead of sweet potato.

 This recipe can be prepared the day before, then reheated.

 Sweet potatoes are excellent baked and roasted as well as boiled.

 Wonderful served with poultry dishes like Braised Duck Legs with Soy, Ginger and Star Anise or Seared Duck Breasts with Balsamic Vinegar, Rosemary and Shallot Sauce (see pages 68 and 74).

celeriac and roasted garlic puree

● Serves: 8   ● Preparation: 10 minutes   ● Cooking: 1 hour

We always look forward to winter because we get to cook root vegetables again. With their earthy sweet flavours, they are wonderful in purees or roasted until crisp. Here we've combined creamy celeriac with nutty roasted garlic to make a classic puree for cold weather.

3 garlic bulbs

3 tbsp olive oil

1 kg (2 lb 4 oz) celeriac, peeled and cut into large chunks

3 tbsp crème fraîche

¼ tsp ground nutmeg

1 tbsp chopped thyme

salt and pepper

chopped parsley to garnish

1 To prepare the garlic puree, preheat the oven to 190°C/375°F/Gas 5. Place the whole garlic bulbs on a large sheet of foil, and drizzle with the olive oil. Seal the foil thoroughly and roast for 1 hour. Then open the foil and allow the garlic to cool a little. Cut the top third off the bulbs and squeeze out all the pulp from each bulb. Discard the skins.

2 Meanwhile, place the celeriac in a saucepan of cold, lightly salted water. Cover, bring to the boil and simmer for about 30 minutes, until tender.

3 Drain the celeriac thoroughly, then place in a food processor with the garlic pulp, crème fraiche, nutmeg, thyme and seasoning. Puree until smooth. Serve hot, sprinkled with chopped parsley.

diva**dos**

 This recipe also works well with parsnip, swede or pumpkin, or try roasted garlic added to mashed potato. It tastes fantastic!

 You can make this the day before, then reheat to serve.

 This puree is excellent served with Slow-roasted Tuscan Pork or Guinea Fowl Breasts with Tarragon (see pages 57 and 70).

diva**don'ts**

 Do not undercook the celeriac. Unlike potatoes, it takes quite a long time to cook through properly.

moroccan carrots

● Serves: 8   ● Preparation: 15 minutes   ● Cooking: 5 minutes

If you've never had this classic North African salad, you are missing out on one of life's greatest pleasures. Baby carrots are bathed in a zesty vinaigrette with copious amounts of paprika, parsley and garlic. They make a great addition to Mezze or can be eaten, slightly mashed, with pitta bread.

750 g (1 lb 10 oz) whole baby carrots, trimmed and peeled

the vinaigrette

125 ml (4 fl oz) extra virgin olive oil

85 ml (3 fl oz) red wine vinegar (Cabernet Sauvignon)

2 tbsp sweet paprika (preferably pimentón)

2 tbsp ground cumin

3 garlic cloves, finely chopped

a small handful of fresh flat-leaf parsley, finely chopped

1 tsp each of salt and pepper

1 To make the vinaigrette, mix together the olive oil, vinegar, paprika, cumin, garlic, parsley, and salt and pepper.

2 Cook the carrots in lightly salted boiling water for 5 minutes until just tender. Drain immediately.

3 Toss the carrots with the vinaigrette and leave to stand at room temperature for 4 hours before serving, or chill overnight.

diva**dos**

If preferred, large carrots can be used and sliced into 5 cm (2 in) batons. If using baby carrots, add a glamorous touch by leaving on a little of the green sprouting top.

Make this salad 1–2 days before your party. This will improve the flavour significantly.

This dish would go well with Lamb Fillet with Roasted Garlic, Coriander and Yogurt Sauce, Salad Mezze Plate, Cumin Flatbread or Filo Tart with Charmoula Chicken (see pages 56, 122, 163 and 52).

diva**don'ts**

Take care not to overcook the carrots, otherwise they will take on a slimy nature.

fennel slaw with dill and cider vinegar dressing

● Serves: 8 ● Preparation: 15 minutes

Too many supermarket delis, with their large tubs of dull coleslaws, have given this salad a seriously downmarket reputation. We've created the new millennium version with wafer thin fennel, dill and a tangy dressing spiked with cider vinegar.

500 g (1 lb 2 oz) fennel bulbs, with cores removed

125 g (4½ oz) red cabbage

1 small red onion, finely chopped

25 g (1 oz) fresh dill, chopped

grated zest of 1 lemon

2 tbsp sugar

1 tsp Tabasco sauce

50 ml (2 fl oz) Classic Mayonnaise (see page 118)

2 tbsp cider vinegar

salt and pepper

1 Using a mandoline or sharp serrated knife, slice the fennel and cabbage as paper-thin as possible, then roughly chop the slices.

2 Combine all the ingredients together and season to taste. Cover and chill for at least 1 hour before serving.

diva**dos**

Choose small white fennel bulbs that are not bruised.

The slaw is best made the day before, improving the flavour and crunchy texture.

Using a mandoline produces stunning results and saves precious Diva time.

Delicious served with Spicy Crab Cakes (see page 84).

diva**don'ts**

Don't substitute dried dill. Fresh dill is an essential flavour in the salad.

baby green salad with beetroot, spring onion, and sesame

● Serves: 8   ● Preparation: 15 minutes

A perfect salad to complement an Oriental or Mediterranean dish and good with grilled meat, fish, or poultry.

3 raw beetroots, peeled

500 g (1 lb 2 oz) selected baby salad leaves

1 bunch of spring onions, trimmed

5 baby red radishes, thinly sliced

2 tbsp toasted sesame seeds to garnish

dressing

2 tbsp rice-wine vinegar

2 tsp light soy sauce

1 tsp sesame oil

½ tsp caster sugar

1 Slice the beetroots into thin slices then cut into fine julienne strips. Toss together the salad leaves, beetroot, spring onions and radishes.

2 Whisk together the rice vinegar, soy sauce, sesame oil and sugar. Pour over the salad just before serving and toss together. Sprinkle over the sesame seeds.

diva**dos**

 Baby spinach, mizuna and rocket leaves are nice for this salad.

 Make the dressing the day before. The salad ingredients can be prepared several hours before serving. Keep covered and chilled. If cutting the beetroot into julienne strips is too time consuming, it can be grated, although this will make the beetroot weep and very wet. Washed salad leaves need to be drained and then well dried in a salad spinner.

caramelized new potatoes with tomato and soy

● Serves: 8　● Preparation: 10 minutes　● Cooking: 45 minutes

This recipe was invented when we were cooking the Roast Fillet of Beef with Coriander and Peanut Pesto (see page 66). It was for a large number of people and required an imaginative and tasty side dish. These potatoes worked perfectly and looked like little glistening jewels on the plate.

1 tbsp light soy sauce

1 tbsp dark soy sauce

1 tbsp honey

1 tbsp olive oil

1 tsp tomato puree

½ tsp English mustard

a pinch of cayenne pepper

750 g (1 lb 10 oz) new potatoes, cleaned

25 g (1 oz) sesame seeds

15 g (½ oz) chives, chopped

1 Preheat the oven to 190ºC/ 375ºF/Gas 5. Mix together the soy sauces, honey, olive oil, tomato puree, mustard, and cayenne pepper. Pour this mixture over the potatoes in a large roasting tin and stir to coat.

2 Place in the oven and roast for 45 minutes, shaking the tin every 15 minutes to prevent sticking. Sprinkle over the sesame seeds 5 minutes before the end of cooking.

3 Remove from the oven and serve sprinkled with chives.

diva**dos**

 Use small round potatoes.

 You can prepare the soy glaze mixture the day before.

 Coat the potatoes with the glaze just before cooking.

 The potatoes are best served hot, straight from the oven. Serve with Roast Fillet of Beef or Miso Glazed Cod (see pages 66 and 92).

diva**don'ts**

 The potatoes should not be wet, or the glaze will slip off and burn on the bottom of the roasting tin.

saffron-roasted potatoes with rosemary and red onions

● Serves: 8   ● Preparation: 10 minutes   ● Cooking: 45 minutes

Show-stopper potatoes, which suit almost any meat or vegetable dish.

1 kg (2 lb 4 oz) large potatoes, peeled

3 red onions, each cut into 6 wedges

saffron dressing

4 tbsp boiling water

a large pinch of saffron powder
or threads

grated zest and juice of 2 lemons

5 tbsp olive oil

85 g (3 oz) butter, diced

1 tsp caster sugar

3 tbsp chopped rosemary
(or 2 tbsp dried)

salt and pepper

1 Preheat the oven to 180°C/ 350°F/Gas 4. Pour boiling water over the saffron and leave to infuse for 5 minutes. Cut the potatoes in half lengthways, then cut each half into three lengthways.

2 In a bowl, mix together the lemon zest and juice, saffron liquid, olive oil, butter, sugar, rosemary and salt and pepper.

3 Place the potatoes and onions in a large roasting tin. Pour over the saffron dressing. Roast for 45 minutes, turning the vegetables every 15 minutes, until tender.

diva**dos**

 Turmeric can be used instead of saffron (use ½ tsp) and fresh or dried thyme can replace the rosemary. You could also use whole shallots instead of red onions.

 The dressing can be prepared several hours ahead, then poured over the potatoes and onions just before roasting.

 Add an extra drizzle of olive oil or water to the potatoes during roasting if they are getting dry but are not quite cooked.

 These potatoes are best served straight from the oven. They are excellent with Butterflied Leg of Lamb with Slow-roasted Tomato, Basil and Olive Confit or Slow-roasted Tuscan Pork (see pages 64 and 57).

fragrant coconut rice

- Serves: 8 - Preparation: 5 minutes - Cooking: 15 minutes

Fluffy rice, enhanced with aromatic cinnamon and rich coconut milk, is a great extra for any Asian meal.

800 ml (28 fl oz) coconut milk (about 2 cans)

125 ml (4 fl oz) water

1 tsp grated lemon zest

1 cinnamon stick

2 tsp salt

450 g (1 lb) basmati or jasmine rice

1 Combine the coconut milk, water, lemon zest, cinnamon stick, and salt in a saucepan and slowly bring to the boil.

2 Stir in the rice and reduce the heat to low. Cover the pan and cook gently for 15 minutes until tender.

3 Stir and check that the rice is cooked. If not, add a little more water and cook for a few more minutes.

4 Take the pan off the heat, remove the cinnamon stick and cover to keep warm until time to serve.

diva**dos**

This recipe can be made a day ahead. Cool, cover and chill until needed. Reheat, covered, in a microwave or steamer to keep the rice moist.

If cooking the rice in advance, then reheating later, do slightly undercook the rice so that it doesn't end up mushy.

Great served with Seared Thai Chicken with Tomato-Chilli Jam, Grilled Indonesian Coconut Chicken or Roasted Winter Vegetables (see pages 80, 18 and 10). The rice looks good served in a large bowl lined with a banana leaf and garnished with large slices of red chilli.

diva**don'ts**

Don't rinse the basmati or jasmine rice for this recipe.

diva**puddings**

sweet goat's cheese, orange, and almond tart

● Serves: 8 ● Preparation: 30 minutes ● Cooking: 35 minutes

Even people who normally dislike goat's cheese will be persuaded! You must try this sumptuous tart, which is especially stunning served warm from the oven with fresh fruit.

250 g (9 oz) sweet shortcrust pastry (see Basic Shortcrust Pastry recipe on page 148, but add 25 g/1 oz caster sugar with the flour and omit the salt and pepper)

the filling

250 g (9 oz) mild soft goat's cheese

250 g (9 oz) cream cheese

125 g (4½ oz) caster sugar

grated zest of ½ orange

½ tsp pure vanilla extract

2 medium eggs, separated

2 tbsp double cream

25 g (1 oz) flaked almonds

1 Preheat the oven to 190°C/375°F/Gas 5. Roll out the pastry and use to line a 20 cm (8 in) loose-bottomed tart tin. Bake blind for 10 minutes (see page 48), then remove the baking beans and bake for a further 5 minutes.

2 Beat the cheeses with the sugar, orange zest, and vanilla until smooth. Add the egg yolks, 1 at a time, and then stir in the cream.

3 Whisk the egg whites until stiff, then fold into the goat's cheese mixture.

4 Pour into the tart shell and scatter the almonds over the surface.

5 Place the tart in the oven and immediately turn the temperature down to 170°C/325°F/Gas 3. Bake for 20 minutes or until just set. (Don't worry if the tart is still a little wobbly – it will set while cooling.)

diva**dos**

 Use a mild, soft goat's cheese, which won't have the strong 'goaty' flavour that the harder ones have.

 This tart can be made a day ahead, then reheated for 10 minutes in a low oven.

 This is excellent in the summer with soft fruits or in the winter with our Winter Glazed Fruits (see page 147). Serve warm or at room temperature.

diva**don'ts**

 Do not chill the cooked tart – the flavour will suffer and the pastry will soften.

honey and mascarpone crème brûlée

- Serves: 8
- Preparation: 20 minutes infusing, several hours chilling, and 20 minutes
- cooking: 45 minutes

Mascarpone and honey gives a crème brûlée a surprising twist. Extremely light and very silky, we think this is the best brûlée ever!

2 medium eggs

3 medium egg yolks

85 g (3 oz) good-quality, fragrant runny honey

300 ml (10 fl oz) milk

300 ml (10 fl oz) double cream

2 vanilla pods, split

1 tbsp grated orange zest

100 g (3½ oz) mascarpone

125 g (4½ oz) caster sugar

1 Preheat the oven to 120°C/ 250°F/Gas ½. Whisk the eggs, egg yolks, and honey in a bowl until pale and thick.

2 Heat the milk, cream, vanilla pods, and orange zest in a saucepan over a medium heat. Remove from heat and leave to infuse for 20 minutes.

3 Remove the vanilla pods and scrape the seeds into the creamy milk. Pour the milk over the egg mixture. Add the mascarpone and whisk gently.

4 Strain the mixture into a large jug, then leave to stand for several hours in the fridge.

5 Pour the custard into 8 ramekins, then place in a large roasting tin and half-fill the tin with hot water. Bake for 40 minutes until just set.

6 Remove and allow to cool, then keep in the fridge until needed.

7 About 30 minutes before serving, spoon the caster sugar over the crèmes in an even layer. Carefully caramelize the tops using a hand-held blow torch.

diva**dos**

 Choose the most flavoursome honey available.

 Make the crèmes the day before. You can 'brûlée' them at least 1 hour before serving.

 If you do not have a blow torch, buy an inexpensive one at a hardware or good kitchen shop! We find overhead grills are too slow – they tend to 'brûlée' the top while melting the base!

 Serve alone or with Winter Glazed Fruits (see page 147), summer fruits or roasted rhubarb. Cut rhubarb into diagonal pieces, place in a non-stick roasting tin, sprinkle with 1–2 tbsp caster sugar and roast at 180°C/350°F/Gas 4 for 5 minutes.

new york cheesecake with fresh blueberries

● Serves: 10 ● Preparation: 4 hours chilling and 15 minutes ● Cooking: 30-40 minutes

Forget about those gelatine-laden cheesecakes. They are sad imposters! This is a full-on cheesecake with a rich, fudgy texture. Excellent with any fresh fruit or eaten all on its lonesome.

base

200 g (7 oz) digestive biscuits, crushed

55 g (2 oz) butter, melted

topping

1 kg (2 lb 4 oz) cream cheese

250 g (9 oz) caster sugar

2 tbsp pure vanilla extract

grated zest and juice of l lemon

5 medium eggs

4 tbsp plain flour

250 g (9 oz) fresh blueberries to decorate

1 Preheat the oven to 180°C/ 350°F/Gas 4. Mix the crushed biscuits with the melted butter. Press firmly into a 20-23 cm (8–9 in) springform tin.

2 Beat the cream cheese and sugar with an electric mixer. Add the vanilla, lemon zest, and juice. Mix until smooth, then add the eggs, one at a time, until fully blended. Add the flour and blend again.

3 Pour the mixture into the tin. Bake for 30-40 minutes until it's firm when jiggled and the top is turning a light golden colour. Rest until cooled, then chill in the fridge for at least 4 hours. Keep the cheesecake in the tin.

4 To serve, remove from the tin and cover the top with the blueberries.

diva**dos**

Use a good-quality cream cheese. Other types of biscuits, like chocolate or ginger, can replace the digestives.

Do make this up to 2 days ahead for the texture to be firm.

Don't worry if a split forms on the top of the cake. This is normal and can be covered with a dusting of icing sugar or fruit.

Serve in thin slices as it's very rich. In the summer, top with red berries and decorate with mint leaves, or in the colder months, top with Winter Glazed Fruits (see page 147).

cinnamon pavlovas with caramelized apples and blackberries

● Serves: 8   ● Preparation: 30 minutes   ● Cooking: 1 hour

Cinnamon and apples are a match made in heaven. We guarantee the unexpected bite into these fragrant pavlovas will give great delight!

meringue

4 medium egg whites

225 g (8 oz) caster sugar

1 tsp cornflour

1 tsp pure vanilla extract

1 tsp white wine vinegar

4 tsp ground cinnamon

topping

3 Granny Smith apples

55 g (2 oz) unsalted butter

115 g (4 oz) soft brown sugar

3 tbsp brandy

100 g (3½ oz) fresh blackberries

250 ml (9 fl oz) double cream

1 Preheat the oven to 180°C/ 350°F/Gas 4. Line 2 baking sheets with greaseproof paper.

2 Whisk the eggs whites until stiff. Gradually whisk in the sugar, a couple of tablespoons at a time, with the cornflour, vanilla, vinegar, and cinnamon, and whisk until smooth and glossy.

3 Divide the meringue mixture evenly on the baking sheets into 8 x 13 cm (5 in) individual circles and make a slight dip in the centres. Place in the oven and immediately turn the oven temperature down to 120°C/ 250°F/Gas ½. Bake for 1 hour, until crisp.

4 Meanwhile, peel, core and cut each apple into 8 thick slices. Gently melt the butter in a saucepan, then add the sugar and stir until dissolved. Add the apples and cook over a medium heat until the apples have softened and caramelized.

5 Just before serving, add the brandy and blackberries to the apples. Whip the cream until stiff.

6 To serve, dollop a spoonful of cream on top of each meringue and spoon over the warm caramelized fruit. Serve immediately.

diva**dos**

 Leave out the cinnamon and you have the classic pavlova recipe.

 Be sure to use egg whites at room temperature, or they will not whisk properly. Make the meringues up to a week before and keep in an airtight container.

 To make 1 large pavlova, divide the mixture into 2 x 20 cm (8 in) round circles. Sandwich together with cream and spoon over the fruit.

 Summer berries would be an excellent alternative fruit in the summer with melted chocolate drizzled over. Use mint leaves or cape gooseberries to decorate and give extra height.

pistachio and berry meringue roulade

● Serves: 8 ● Preparation: 20 minutes ● Cooking: 15 minutes

We've turned the old, reliable meringue, into something quite sublime. Berries and cream are rolled with chewy, nutty meringue for this terrific party pudding.

5 medium egg whites

pinch of salt

250 g (9 oz) caster sugar

100 g (3½ oz) unsalted, shelled pistachio nuts, coarsely chopped

300 ml (10 fl oz) double cream

200 g (7 oz) fresh raspberries

sifted icing sugar and summer berries to decorate

1 Preheat the oven to 170°C/325°F/Gas 3. Line a 25 x 35 cm (10 x 14 in) Swiss roll tin with greaseproof paper.

2 Whisk the egg whites with the salt until stiff. Gradually whisk in the sugar, a couple of tablespoons at a time. Fold in the pistachio nuts, then spread the mixture evenly in the tin. Bake for 15 minutes, until crisp on the outside. Remove from the oven and cool.

3 Whip the cream until stiff, then gently fold in the raspberries.

4 Turn the meringue out on to another sheet of greaseproof paper, and then carefully peel away the lining paper.

5 Spread the berry cream evenly over the meringue, then roll up lengthways. Dust with icing sugar and decorate with berries.

diva**dos**

 Any soft fruit, fruit curd or berries can be used in the filling. A mixture of Greek yogurt with cream is also delicious. You can buy unsalted, shelled pistachio nuts in the baking section of most supermarkets.

 Make the meringue a day ahead. Fill and roll, and keep in the fridge up to 6 hours before serving.

 Do not cook the meringue for more than 20 minutes – over-cooking will make it hard to roll. Don't worry if the meringue is not crisping up – it will once removed from the oven.

 If liked, serve with a berry coulis.

winter glazed fruits

● Serves: 8   ● Preparation: 10 minutes   ● Cooking: 15 minutes

Winter fruits are perfect for glazing with butter, brown sugar and brandy, especially if you have under-ripe fruit. Serve with crisp, nutty biscotti and crème fraîche.

4 Granny Smith apples

3 Conference pears

4 firm dark plums

55 g (2 oz) unsalted butter

115 g (4 oz) soft brown sugar or caster sugar

2 tbsp Armagnac or brandy

1 Peel the apples and pears, core and cut into thick slices. Halve the plums, remove the stones, and cut into quarters.

2 Melt the butter in a large frying pan, add the sugar, and stir a little to dissolve the sugar, allowing the sugar to darken a little.

3 Then add the apples and pears. Cook, stirring, for 5 minutes, or until the fruit has begun to soften. Add the plums and continue cooking gently for 3–5 minutes, until the fruit has glazed and softened.

4 Just before serving, add the Armagnac or brandy.

diva**dos**

The fruit must be firm or it will cook to a mush. This recipe is also excellent with firm sweet apricots, when in season.

This can be cooked ahead of time, then gently reheated to serve.

Serve with crème fraîche, Greek yogurt or ice-cream and biscotti or your favourite biscuits.

puddings and baking ingredients

Rich, creamy, and fragrant, that's what most pudding ingredients are all about. Core ingredients aside, they are responsible for the oohs and aahs when people tuck in! Quality and freshness are paramount, and please don't consider reduced-fat versions of dairy products – their flavour is inferior and they can alter the consistency of a pudding.

CORE INGREDIENTS

Butter: We prefer salted butter for its creamy flavour, unless unsalted butter is specified. Butter freezes well or stores in the fridge for several weeks. Margarine should be avoided at all costs.

Flour: We recommend using Italian 00 flour for all our pastry recipes. You'll need strong plain flour for bread-making, ordinary plain flour for sauces and self-raising flour for cakes and scones.

Eggs: Eggs should be as fresh as possible and should be kept in the fridge. Remove and allow them to stand at room temperature for 10 minutes before using. When making meringues, it is imperative that the eggs are not cold or the whites will not whisk properly. We use medium eggs unless otherwise stated.

Sugar: Caster sugar is the most useful sugar, but granulated can be ground finer in a food processor. Muscovado and soft brown sugars are from unrefined cane sugar and provide lovely colour and flavour. Sifted icing sugar is excellent dusted over hot and cold puddings.

CREAMS, YOGURTS AND CREAM CHEESES

Double Cream: Behind clotted cream, this has one of the highest fat contents – some 48 per cent. The higher the fat, the more sturdy it is when whipped. This rich, thick cream is used for cooking and whipping, and is excellent for roulades, meringues and pouring over puddings. Mix with soft fruits, curds, melted chocolate, vanilla, or liqueurs for more flavour.

Single Cream: Best used for topping hot puddings, adding to soups, hot drinks, or sauces.

Whipping Cream: Similar to double cream but with a lower fat content of around 35 per cent. When whisked it produces a light, airy texture, ideal for cream-based puddings. Less expensive than double cream, it's useful when a large quantity is required.

Soured Cream: This runny, sour-flavoured cream is similar to crème fraîche. A simple fruit tart can be made with a mixture of soured cream, sugar, eggs, orange zest, and fresh berries poured into a tart shell and baked for 30 minutes.

Crème Fraîche: Created by adding buttermilk, soured cream, or yogurt to cream. Crème fraîche is rich and creamy with a slight tang. It's superb served with fruit tarts and chocolate cakes. As it's a cultured product, it doesn't curdle when boiled, so it's a useful cooking cream. It keeps well in the fridge.

Greek Yogurt: This thick and creamy yogurt is one of our favourite ingredients. It has a lovely sharp flavour, which lends itself to desserts and is divine with fruit. Also wonderful with many savoury dishes.

Mascarpone Cheese: The key ingredient of tiramisu, this delicious Italian cheese is made by curdling thick cream. It has a sweetish flavour and can be used to replace cream. Serve with tarts, poached pears or chocolate cakes. It also makes fantastic crème brûlée and ice-cream.

Mild Goat's Cheese: A light, creamy-textured cheese that's far milder than the drier, rinded variety and very versatile. You can buy either English or French. We like the variety sold in small tubs, which keeps well in the fridge. If goat's cheese is unavailable, then cream cheese can be used as a substitute in many recipes.

Cream Cheese: Simply luscious for cheesecakes but excellent for a range of sweet dishes.

Fromage Frais: Although used in the same way as yogurt and cream, fromage frais is actually a cheese. It can replace yogurt but it doesn't heat well so it is used mainly in cold dishes.

CHOCOLATE

White Chocolate: This contains no cocoa solids, so it has a pale appearance and mild, sweet taste. It's good for biscuits and useful for coating and decorating. White chocolate burns easily, so melt gently over simmering water.

Dark Chocolate: Trying to figure out exactly what kind of chocolate to purchase can be confusing, but we believe that price is generally a good indicator of quality. It should contain a high percentage of cocoa solids, the higher the better, and this figure is usually stated on the label. Top quality is around 75 per cent cocoa solids and has an intensely chocolatey flavour, ideal for rich desserts. Bittersweet, semisweet or baking chocolates have a lesser cocoa butter content and therefore lower quality, but can still produce good desserts.

CITRUS FRUITS

Oranges, lemons, limes, and grapefruit are essential ingredients in dessert-making, and should be used both for flavouring and garnishing. Orange and pink grapefruit segments can look stunning with mint for decorating a meringue or cake, grated zests are lovely in pastry, and citrus fruit juices are wonderful mixed with cream and eggs for a tart filling.

NUTS

Nuts are tasty for all cooking, but they are especially good for baking and desserts. We find almonds, hazelnuts, pistachio nuts, pine nuts, and walnuts the most useful. For an intense flavour, roast and grind your own: scatter the nuts on a baking tray and place in a moderately hot oven for 8–10 minutes until golden. Cool, then grind in a food processor. Home-made praline with hazelnuts, pine nuts or almonds is delicious and can be crushed and added to ice-cream.

VANILLA

Vanilla pods are the dried, seed cases of a tropical orchid and have a most fragrant aroma. Although expensive, pods can be washed, dried and re-used several times and blended with sugar. The pods are mainly used for flavouring creams and liquids, and then removed after infusing. For extra flavour, add the seeds – cut the pod open lengthways and scrape out the seeds with the tip of a knife. Pure vanilla essence is created by extracting the flavour from the pods with alcohol. It is commonly used in cakes, cookies, and biscuits, and should be used sparingly, as it has a strong flavour. Vanilla extract is milder and more diluted, and, like essence, it is sold in a liquid form.

double chocolate mascarpone tart

● Serves: 8–10   ● Preparation: 30 minutes chilling and 20 minutes   ● Cooking: 50 minutes

What could be a more decadent combination than a flaky chocolate crust and a creamy filling of mascarpone and dark chocolate? A deliciously tempting pudding for serious chocoholics!

chocolate pastry

150 g (5½ oz) plain flour

1 tbsp icing sugar

2 tbsp dark cocoa powder

100 g (3½ oz) salted butter, chilled

1 medium egg

filling

200 g (7 oz) dark chocolate, broken into pieces

600 g (1 lb 5 oz) mascarpone

150 g (5½ oz) caster sugar

3 medium eggs

1 tbsp brandy

1 Preheat the oven to 180°C/ 350°F/Gas 4.

2 To make the pastry, place the flour, sugar, cocoa powder, and butter in a food processor and blend until the mixture resembles fine breadcrumbs. Add the egg and mix briefly to form a firm dough.

3 Roll out the pastry thinly on a lightly floured surface. Use to line a 20 cm (8 in) loose-bottomed, deep tart tin. Prick the pastry base several times with a fork. Chill for 30 minutes.

4 Place a piece of greaseproof paper in the tart shell, fill with baking beans and bake blind for 10 minutes. Remove the beans and paper, and bake for another 5 minutes.

5 Remove the tart shell and reduce the oven temperature to 150°C/ 300°F/Gas 2.

6 For the filling, begin by melting the chocolate in a bowl over a pan of simmering water or in a microwave on medium power.

7 Beat the mascarpone with the sugar and eggs. Divide the mixture between 2 bowls and add the melted chocolate to one half and the brandy to the other.

8 Spoon each mixture alternatively into the tart shell so that it will be layered all through. Bake at the same temperature for 35 minutes or until just set. Chill for 2 hours before serving.

diva**dos**

If mascarpone is not available, use cream cheese. Use good quality, dark cocoa powder for the pastry.

Make the day before serving and keep covered in a cool place.

Don't worry if the filling takes a while to set. It's best cooked at a low oven temperature.

Serve with summer berries or a sharp berry coulis. It doesn't need more cream for pouring over!

pineapple tarte tatin with star anise

● Serves: 8   ● Preparation: 20 minutes   ● Cooking: 30-35 minutes

Tarte tatin can be made with almost any fruit. Our friend Julie, a brilliant pudding-maker, inspired us with this luscious combination of fresh pineapple, star anise, and caramel on flaky puff pastry.

200 g (7 oz) puff pastry

85 g (3 oz) caster sugar

40 g (1½ oz) unsalted butter

2 star anise, crushed in a spice mill

½ tsp ground cinnamon

1 vanilla pod, split and scraped

1 large fresh pineapple (weighing about 900 g (2 lb), peeled, cored, and sliced into 5 mm (¼ in) pieces

1 Preheat the oven to 190°C/ 375°F/Gas 5. Roll out the pastry to a 25 cm (10 in) round, so that it's slightly larger than a 20 cm (8 in) tart tin (not loose-bottomed) or tarte tatin tin. (Alternatively, you can make 8 individual tarts in tart tins lined with greaseproof paper.)

2 To make the caramel, heat the sugar and butter together in a saucepan, stirring a little at first until the sugar has dissolved. Then cook, without stirring, until it forms a bubbling golden caramel. Stir in the crushed star anise, cinnamon, and the vanilla seeds and pod. Pour the caramel into the tin.

3 Place the pineapple evenly over the base of the tart tin or divide evenly among the individual tart tins. Bake for 12 minutes.

4 Remove tart(s) from the oven and place the pastry on top, tucking the edges down the sides. Prick 6 times with a fork and bake for another 20 minutes, until the pastry is crisp and golden.

5 Cool for at least 5 minutes, then invert the tart(s) on to a plate. Remove the vanilla pod.

diva**dos**

 Make the day before and reheat for 10–15 minutes in a moderately hot oven before serving.

 Perfect little non-stick tarte tatin tins are available in good kitchenware shops.

 Serve warm as the grand finale to an Asian or Indian meal. It's delicious with either cream or crème fraîche.

diva**don'ts**

 Don't buy a ripe pineapple that is too soft, as it may have rotten spots in it.

fresh fig and plum tarte tatin with hot fudge sauce

● Serves: 8   ● Preparation: 25 minutes   ● Cooking: 40 minutes

This pudding boasts stunning dark purple colours with autumn flavours. Delicious made individually or as a whole tart.

8 firm dark plums, halved and stoned

55 g (2 oz) unsalted butter

115 g (4 oz) caster sugar plus 1 tbsp extra

200 g (7 oz) puff pastry

16 fresh figs, halved and cored

1 tsp ground cinnamon

fudge sauce

75 g (2¾ oz) light soft brown sugar

55 g (2 oz) unsalted butter

3 tbsp double cream

1 Preheat the oven to 190°C/ 375°F/Gas 5.

2 Place the plums on a baking tray, dot with 25 g (1 oz) of the butter and sprinkle over 25 g (1 oz) of the sugar. Bake for 20 minutes until soft.

3 Roll the pastry out thinly and cut out 8 x 10 cm (4 in) circles with a large biscuit cutter. Or, if making one large tart, use a large dinner plate for cutting around. Chill until needed.

4 Melt the remaining butter and the remaining weighed amount of caster sugar together in a saucepan, stirring a little until the sugar has dissolved. Then cook, without stirring, until it forms a bubbling golden caramel. Pour immediately into 8 individual tarte tatin tins, 8 ramekins or 1 large tart tin (not loose-bottomed).

5 Place the figs, cut side down, on top of the caramel, and press down firmly. Sprinkle with cinnamon and the extra 1 tbsp sugar. Place 2 plums halves in each tart or arrange evenly in the large tart.

6 Top the tarts with the chilled pastry rounds, tucking the edges down the sides so as to create a rim when the tart(s) is inverted. Prick 6 times with a fork. Place on a large baking tray and bake for 20 minutes until crisp and golden.

7 Place all the ingredients for the sauce in a saucepan and bring to the boil, whisking to combine.

8 Invert the tart(s) out on to warm plates and serve with the hot fudge sauce.

diva**dos**

This recipe is best made in late summer or autumn, when figs are in season and plums are sweet but firm.

The tart(s) can be made the day before, then reheated for 15 minutes in a moderately hot oven. This works well, as the colour improves and they become a little firmer, so are easier to turn out and serve.

This tart is extra delicious also served with crème fraîche.

chocolate and amaretti meringue roulade

● Serves: 8 ● Preparation: 15 minutes ● Cooking: 15 minutes

This sounds quintessentially Christmassy, but is actually so versatile that you can serve it all year round. It tastes wonderful with summer berries and is a chocolate lover's dream.

meringue

5 medium egg whites

a pinch of salt

250 g (9 oz) caster sugar

3 tbsp dark cocoa powder, sifted

filling

250 ml (9 fl oz) double cream

85 g (3 oz) amaretti biscuits, crushed

3 tbsp amaretto liqueur or brandy

1 Preheat the oven to 160°C/ 325°F/Gas 3. Line a 25 x 35 cm (10 x 14 in) Swiss roll tin with greaseproof paper.

2 Whisk the egg whites with the salt until stiff, then gradually whisk in the sugar, a couple of tablespoons at a time. Fold in the cocoa powder. Spread the meringue mixture evenly in the tin.

3 Bake for 15 minutes until crispy on the outside. Remove from the oven and cool.

4 Whip the cream until stiff, then fold in the crushed biscuits and liqueur or brandy.

5 Turn the meringue out on to another sheet of greaseproof paper and carefully peel away the lining paper. Spread the cream mixture over the meringue and roll up lengthways. Chill until ready to serve.

diva**dos**

 Chopped stem ginger can be used instead of the amaretti biscuits. Use 3 pieces, drained of syrup, and finely chop.

 Follow the golden rules of whisking egg whites: use room temperature egg whites and a clean bowl to whisk them in, otherwise they will not thicken properly. The meringue can be made the day before, but fill and roll the roulade on the day of serving the dessert.

 The meringue should be crispy when removed from the oven. If it's not, do not cook further, otherwise it will not roll well. It will crisp as it cools down.

 Serve with caramelised pears (follow the recipe for Winter Glazed Fruits on page 147) and decorate with cape gooseberries. In the summer, the roulade is excellent drizzled with melted white chocolate and decorated with fresh berries.

chez panisse chocolate cake

● Serves: 8   ● Preparation: 20 minutes   ● Cooking: 25-30 minutes

Over the past years at Books for Cooks, there has always been a quest to find the perfect chocolate cake. We must have tried at least 50 different recipes, but always came back to this one. The famous Chez Panisse restaurant outside San Francisco is the creator of this fabulous recipe. It is the richest, most squidgy chocolate cake you will ever have.

250 g (9 oz) dark chocolate, broken into pieces

250 g (9 oz) salted butter

6 medium eggs, separated

½ tsp cream of tartar

175 g (6 oz) caster sugar

55 g (2 oz) light soft brown sugar

55 g (2 oz) ground almonds

3 tbsp plain flour, sifted

sifted icing sugar and/or cocoa powder to decorate

1 Preheat the oven to 190°C/ 375°F/Gas 5. Grease the base and line with greaseproof paper a 20–23 cm (8–9 in) springform cake tin. Dust with a little flour.

2 Melt the chocolate and butter in a bowl over a pan of simmering water or in a microwave on medium power. Once melted, whisk together until smooth.

3 Whisk the egg whites and cream of tartar with an electric mixer until soft peaks form.

4 Whisk the egg yolks in a large mixing bowl with both the sugars until thick and pale. Pour in the chocolate mixture, and gently mix until smooth.

5 Add the almonds and flour to the chocolate mixture and mix again. Carefully fold in the egg whites.

6 Pour the batter into the prepared tin. Bake for 25–30 minutes until the cake is set but slightly wobbly in the centre. Cool in the tin.

7 To serve, run a knife around the edge and remove the cake from the tin. Peel off the paper and place on a cake platter. Dust with icing sugar and/or cocoa powder.

diva**dos**

 Buy a good-quality dark chocolate. We are great fans of Bournville for flavour and reliability.

 The cake can be made up to 3 days before the party. Use eggs at room temperature. Make sure that your mixer bowl is spotlessly clean, or the egg whites will not whisk properly.

 Serve with crème fraîche, mascarpone or home-made ice-cream. This cake is delectably rich, so keep portions small.

diva**don'ts**

 Don't refrigerate the cake if making ahead. Simply place foil over the top and leave at room temperature.

heavenly chunky-chewy chocolate cookies

• Makes: 30 • Preparation: 20 minutes • Cooking: 10 minutes

Why not just double the quantity now, because you'll never have enough! The most difficult thing about preparing these cookies is trying not to eat them before they're due to be served!

125 g (4½ oz) plain flour

25 g (1 oz) dark cocoa powder

½ tsp bicarbonate of soda

a pinch of salt

125 g (4½ oz) dark chocolate, broken into pieces

85 g (3 oz) unsalted butter

175 g (6 oz) soft brown sugar

2 small eggs

1 tsp pure vanilla extract

350 g (12 oz) dark chocolate chips

55 g (2 oz) white chocolate, broken into pieces

1 Preheat the oven to 180°C/ 350°F/Gas 4. Sift together into a bowl the flour, cocoa powder, bicarbonate of soda, and salt.

2 Gently melt the dark chocolate in a bowl over a pan of simmering water or in a microwave on medium power.

3 Cream the butter and sugar together until light and fluffy, then beat in the eggs, vanilla, and melted chocolate.

4 Stir the chocolate chips and white chocolate pieces into the creamed mixture, mix well, then add the flour mixture. Stir well together.

5 Line 3–4 large baking trays with greaseproof paper and place 30 heaped tablespoons of the cookie mixture onto the tray. Bake for 10 minutes.

6 Cool slightly for several minutes on the tray then remove with a fish slice or palette knife and cool on a wire rack.

diva**dos**

Milk and dark chocolate chips are readily available, but white chocolate chunks are better than using white chocolate chips.

These are best made on the day of eating, but can be made several days before. Store in an airtight container. Reheat in a very low oven for just 5 minutes, if you like them slightly soft and chewy.

Do not overcook – better to undercook as they should be soft and chewy!

Serve on their own or with berries and cream or ice-cream.

diva**breads**

diva breadsticks

- Makes: 25 breadsticks
- cooking: 20 minutes
- Preparation: 1 hour proving and 30 minutes

Try our basic Olive Oil and Sea Salt Bread (see page 160) twisted with the lusty fillings listed below. You can serve these breadsticks warm.

FILLINGS

garlic and rosemary confit

3 garlic bulbs, unpeeled

3 tbsp olive oil

50 ml (2 fl oz) balsamic vinegar

1 tbsp chopped rosemary

½ tsp each salt and pepper

parmesan, red onion, and prosciutto

2 tbsp olive oil

2 red onions, thickly sliced

½ tsp each of salt and pepper

25 thin slices of proscuitto, diced

50 g (1¾ oz) Parmesan cheese, grated

olive, chilli, and fennel seed

100 g (3½ oz) pitted Italian black olives, chopped

2 tbsp fennel seeds

1 tsp crushed dried red chillies

1 tbsp each of salt and pepper

1 Preheat the oven to 200°C/400°F/Gas 6.

2 Follow the basic recipe for Olive Oil and Sea Salt Bread (page 160). After proving, when the bread dough has doubled in size, knock back the dough and knead for 2 minutes, then roll out into a large square. Spread your chosen filling (see below) over one half and fold the dough over. Press down with your fingertips. Slice the dough into 25 long, thin slices. Roll each slice back and forth with the palms of your hands and then twist the ends in an opposite direction.

3 Place the sticks on baking sheets covered with baking paper, sprinkle with salt and pepper and bake for 20 minutes until golden brown. Then cool.

garlic and rosemary confit

Blanch the garlic cloves for 3 minutes in boiling water. Drain and refresh under cold running water. Peel each clove. Heat the oil in a medium saucepan and lightly brown the garlic. Add the vinegar, rosemary, salt and pepper, and 4 tbsp water. Cook gently for 3 minutes till the mixture is syrupy.

parmesan, red onion, and prosciutto

Heat the olive oil in a frying pan, add the onions and salt and pepper; fry until soft, then place in a bowl with the prosciutto and Parmesan.

olive, chilli, and fennel seed

Mix the ingredients together in a small bowl.

diva**dos**

Use good quality olives. Remove any excess fat from the prosciutto.

Prepare the breadstick fillings the day ahead, but try to bake the sticks fresh to serve.

olive oil and sea salt bread

- Preparation: 1 hour proving and 10 minutes
- Cooking: 20 minutes

We have always had a love-hate relationship with making bread. Sometimes it worked and other times not! It wasn't until we went to the organic bakery in Penrith for a weekend that we sorted ourselves out. This is one of the most simple and foolproof of recipes for making bread. It doesn't require any bigas, sourdough starters or lengthy proving time. Use this master recipe for most of the breads in this chapter.

25 g (1 oz) dried yeast

a pinch of sugar

450 ml (16 fl oz) tepid water

900 g (2 lb) strong white (bread) flour, preferably organic

1 tsp sea salt

150 ml (5 fl oz) olive oil

1 Stir the yeast and sugar into the tepid water and leave for 5–10 minutes, until it starts to froth.

2 Combine the flour and salt in a large bowl, then add the olive oil and yeast liquid. Mix with a large wooden spoon or your hands to bring together into a soft, springy dough. Remove from the bowl and place on to a lightly floured surface. Knead for 5 minutes until you have a smooth, elastic dough. If the dough feels heavy and dry, add a drop more water to it and keep kneading.

3 Place the dough in a large, lightly oiled bowl and cover tightly with clingfilm. Leave to rise in a draught-free place for 1 hour or until doubled in size. Take the dough out and knead for a few minutes.

4 Follow individual recipes from here.

diva**dos**

 One of the reasons bread can have a close texture is because the dough was lacking in moisture. The stiffness keeps it from rising properly, so add a little more water but not too much as this can make the bread heavy.

 Having a warm environment for the dough to prove is ideal. If your house is cold and draughty, heat your oven to 130°C/250°F/ Gas ½ for 5 minutes. Turn off and place the covered bowl of bread inside. Leave to rise for the required time.

miniature focaccia topped with caramelized onions

- Makes: about 25 mini breads   • Preparation: 20 minutes   • Cooking: 45 minutes

Irresistible little flavoured breads, which are ideal for parties.

1 quantity Olive Oil and Sea Salt Bread (see page 160)

topping

3 red onions, cut into wedges

4 tbsp olive oil

2 tbsp balsamic vinegar

15 g (½ oz) butter

sea salt and pepper

rosemary or thyme sprigs

1 Preheat the oven to 190°C/375°F/Gas 5. Place the onions in a roasting tin, drizzle with oil and vinegar, dot with butter, and season with salt and pepper. Roast for 30 minutes, shaking a couple of times during cooking.

2 Follow the basic method for the Olive Oil Bread (page 160), until it has proven and doubled in size.

3 Increase the oven temperature to 220°C/425°F/Gas 7. Turn the dough out on to a lightly floured surface and divide into about 25 x 55 g (2 oz) pieces. Briefly shape into rounds, then press each ball down with your fingertips. Place the mini focaccia on 2 lightly oiled baking trays.

4 Top each bread with some of the caramelized onions and a herb sprig, then scatter a little sea salt over. Bake for 15 minutes, or until the bread sounds hollow when tapped underneath. Place on a wire rack to cool. Serve warm or at room temperature.

diva**dos**

 Use good-quality strong plain (bread) flour for making the dough. Other strong-flavoured herbs such as sage can be used and, if desired, try placing a small piece of blue cheese on to the bread, pushing it into the dough under the onions.

 Do cover the dough properly when rising, as draughts can inhibit the rising process. If more convenient, make the dough the night before and leave it in the fridge to rise overnight. Bring back to room temperature before shaping.

cumin flatbread

● Makes: 2 loaves   ● Preparation: 1 hour proving and 15 minutes   ● Cooking: 15 minutes

This spicy garlic bread has a brilliant yellow colour and tasty bits of cumin in every bite.

500 g (1 lb 2 oz) strong white (bread) flour

1 tbsp salt

2 tbsp cumin seeds, toasted and crushed

25 g (1 oz) fresh yeast or 15 g (½ oz) dried yeast

pinch of sugar

250 ml (9 fl oz) tepid water

90 ml (3 fl oz) olive oil

2 garlic cloves, finely chopped

1 tsp turmeric

25 g (1 oz) fresh coriander, chopped

1 Put the flour, salt, and toasted cumin seeds in a large bowl. Dissolve the yeast and sugar in the warm water and leave for 5 minutes, until frothy. Warm the olive oil in a small pan and add the garlic, turmeric and coriander. Leave the garlic to soften slightly for 5 minutes, then remove the pan from the heat. Leave to cool.

2 Add the cooled oil to the flour mixture, pour over the yeasted water and mix into a smooth dough with your hands. Knead for about 5 minutes on a lightly floured work surface until the dough is smooth and elastic and no longer sticky.

3 Place the dough in a lightly oiled bowl, cover with clingfilm or a tea-towel and leave in a draught-free place for 1 hour or until doubled in size.

4 Preheat the oven to 220°C/ 425°F/Gas mark 7.

5 Knock back the dough, knead again for a few minutes, then roll out on a lightly floured surface into 2 x 18 cm (7 in) flat circles. Place on 2 greased baking trays and allow to rest for 5 minutes.

6 Bake for 15 minutes, until the loaves sound hollow when tapped underneath. Leave to cool on wire racks.

diva**dos**

 You can vary the herbs and spices used for this bread.

 You can make the dough a day ahead, then leave it to proof overnight. Bring back to room temperature before continuing.

 Do ensure that the oven is properly preheated.

 Serve with Salad Mezze Plate, Spicy Prawns with Moroccan Tomato Jam and Filo Tart with Charmoula Chicken (see pages 122, 27 and 52). You can make lots of little spiced flatbreads instead of 2 large ones. Bake for 15 minutes.

diva**cooking**

herbs and spices

What would the world be without herbs and spices? Pretty boring. Home-grown herbs fresh from your garden are invaluable, or visit markets to find large bunches. Dried spices go stale after six months, so check use-by dates.

SOUTHEAST ASIAN HERBS

Coriander: This gorgeous herb lends itself to most highly seasoned food. The roots and stems are essential for curry pastes and the leaves for salads, curries, salsas, and sauces.

Galangal: Similar to its cousin ginger, galangal is prepared in the same way. It has a medicinal odour that works in curry pastes and coconut milk soups.

Lemongrass: Prized for its lime and lemon flavour in Thai soups, salads, and curries. Use the lower bottom piece, which is the most tender part. Crush the stem with a knife and peel away the outer layers. Finely chop the remainder for Oriental stocks or teas. Lemongrass freezes well.

Lime Leaves: These aromatic leaves from the Thai kaffir lime tree add a lemony flavour to soups, curries, and salads. Finely julienne the leaves for salads; leave whole for other dishes. They freeze well, but lose their colour.

Thai Sweet Basil: Related to Italian basil, the Thai variety looks similar but is more aromatic, adding a distinctive flavour to salads and soups. Keep basil wrapped in wet kitchen paper and chilled, as it goes off quickly.

MEDITERRANEAN and MIDDLE EASTERN HERBS

Basil: There is no other aroma like a whiff of pungent basil. It can transform tomatoes and salads, taking them to a whole new level.

Flat-leaf Parsley: Almost considered a vegetable in the Middle East as it's used so often. Superior to the curly variety, it is de rigueur for Mediterranean salads, sauces, and meats. Use the stems for stock and in bouquet garnis.

Mint: There are more than 200 varieties, but spearmint has the best taste. It's great in salads, marinades and herb sauces as well as cool drinks.

Oregano: This herb pairs well with tomatoes, poultry, and meats. Use sparingly as the flavour is powerful.

Rosemary: Excellent with meats, fish, poultry, and beans. The needles should be finely chopped and the stems can be used for barbecue skewers (see page 20).

Sage: Used mainly by the Italians, it's delicious deep-fried on ravioli, pasta, risotto, poultry, or game dishes, and is key for stuffings and roasts.

Tarragon: An assertive French herb, classically used for Béarnaise Sauce and Remoulade Mayonnaise. It's lovely with poultry, fish and cold meats and makes a dreamy partner for tomatoes.

DRIED SPICES

ITALIAN

Fennel Seed: With its sweet liquorice flavour, whole fennel seed complements salads, vegetables, roasts, and breads. When crushed, it can add a subtle taste to risottos or pastas.

Saffron: An expensive spice, thankfully used in small amounts! We prefer saffron threads as they hold their flavour for longer. Powdered saffron can be deceptive as it's often adulterated. To draw out more flavour and colour, infuse saffron in 2 tbsp boiling water before using.

CHINESE

Five Spice: A pungent dry spice made from cinnamon, cloves, fennel, star anise, and Szechwan peppercorns. It's excellent with roast pork and duck and wonderful when sprinkled on Asian roast vegetables.

Star Anise: Used mostly with poultry, game and fruit puddings, this spice infuses an exotic liquorice taste. Leave whole or finely grind in a spice mill.

INDIAN AND ASIAN SPICES

Cardamom: A spicy-sweet aromatic that adds a lovely flavour to stews, curries and chutneys, but also works well used subtly in cream. Crush in a mortar and pestle, discarding the pods, to leave the seeds..

Cinnamon: This sweet, fragrant spice enhances all puddings, tagines and stews. Grind your own sticks for the freshest flavour and use whole sticks to infuse mulled wines and fruit punches.

Coriander Seeds: Popular since ancient times, coriander's spicy taste complements meats and vegetables. Toasting and grinding the seeds is effortless and makes a big flavour difference.

Cumin: A popular and extremely versatile spice. The nutty, peppery seeds can be ground with other spices for curries, or used whole with vegetables and meats.

Ground Ginger: Very different to its fresh form and mostly used in Indian curries and North African tagines. It's a key flavouring in curry spice mixtures and also works well in tarts, cakes, and hot puddings.

Turmeric: Widely used in curries and tagines, turmeric provides a powerful flavour and brilliant colour. It's lovely with root vegetables such as potatoes or to brighten up rice – just add to the cooking water.

LATIN AMERICAN AND OTHER GROUND CHILLI SPICES

Chilli Powder: The key flavour in beef or black bean chilli, this is made from ground dried chillies. Great for grilled meats or vegetables in tortilla wraps.

Crushed Red Chillies: When that extra kick is needed, this is the all-purpose spice to do the job. Pasta, seafood and chicken as well as salads taste perfect with a little heat added.

Ground Cayenne Pepper: For more subtle heat, add cayenne by the pinch. It's especially good added to potato or crab cakes.

Paprika: The Hungarian variety is considered to be the best and varies from mild and sweet to hot. Our favourite is the Spanish pimentón, which has a smoky aroma. It complements seafood, sauces, salsas, meats, stews, and rice dishes.

strong ethnic flavours

Go to any ethnic supermarket and you'll find an Aladdin's cave of exotic ingredients. If you live in a remote area, many shops do mail order, or browse the internet to find speciality companies and buy more unusual items online.

ITALIAN

Capers: Add a piquant salty flavour to any dish. Those packed in salt are superior to brined, but do soak them before using. When teamed with their soulmate, anchovies, capers have a magical depth. Excellent in fish or poultry dishes.

Caperberries: Popular as an antipasti component or baked with poultry, caperberries could soon replace olives as your favourite snack. They are left on the caper shrub longer than capers, producing a seedy texture inside.

Olives: For recipes, look for the dark black variety mixed with olive oil and herbs – they are mild in flavour and won't overpower the dish. Please don't use canned. Fortunately it is now possible to buy good quality, pitted olives.

Dried Mushrooms: Italian porcini and French ceps add a huge flavour dimension to meat and poultry dishes. Soak for 20 minutes in boiling water and use the soaking liquid as stock. Rinse well before using, as they can be quite sandy.

Saba: A new ingredient to come on the market, which dates back to Roman times. It is prepared from concentrated grape musk and is fantastic in sauces for game and poultry, and in salad dressings.

CHINESE

Hoisin Sauce: Made from soya beans, garlic and chillies, this sweet and spicy sauce is a boost for Asian marinades and sauces.

Soy Sauce: This dark salty sauce complements any Asian dish. We prefer the light Japanese soy sauce to the dark, which can be too heavy and salty.

Sweet Chilli Bean Paste: Gorgeous sauce made from fermented soya beans or black beans, chillies, and garlic. It is essential for peanut dipping sauces and noodle dishes.

JAPANESE

Saké: Made from rice, saké is not only Japan's favourite alcohol, it's also used in cooking for sauces and marinades and for toning down strong flavours.

Mirin: A milder, thicker version of saké, mirin adds a lovely sweetness to Asian sauces, dressings, marinades and glazes. It's particularly great in dressings for noodle salads, chicken, or fish.

Miso Paste: The peanut butter of Japan, miso is made from fermented soya beans. There are 3 varieties available – yellow, red, and brown. Use the lighter colours for soups and sauces, and the dark for heavy dishes. Miso is excellent in Asian marinades, vinaigrettes and glazes.

THAI

Fish Sauce (Nam Pla): This is used in just about everything in southeast Asia. Made of fermented anchovies, this essential sauce imparts a salty, pungent and sharp taste to dressings, sauces and curries. When paired with lime juice, sugar, and chillies, it's pure magic.

Sweet Chilli Dipping Sauce: This syrupy condiment made of chilli, garlic, sugar, and rice wine vinegar is the perfect dipping sauce – delicious with fried foods, Thai salads, or mixed with coconut milk for sauces. It is honestly better in a bottle than making your own!

Tom Yum Paste: Made of chillies, galangal (like ginger), lemongrass, and lime leaves, we love this spicy, hot and sour-tasting paste in Asian curries, soups, and sauces.

KOREAN

Kochujang: A sweet and spicy chilli paste that's superb in marinades for beef, poultry, or seafood. Best found in Japanese or Korean food shops.

Sesame Oil: Fantastic for its nutty smoky flavour, and great for marinades, dressings, and stir-fries. Do not keep for too long or it will lose its beautiful fragrance.

INDONESIAN

Ketchap Manis: This dark seductive soy sauce is thicker and sweeter than its Chinese cousin. Use as a condiment for canapés or stir-fried with noodles, and add to sauces and salsas.

Sambal Oelek: A lovely concentrated mixture of chillies, brown sugar and salt. It makes a brilliant shortcut for any recipe using chopped fresh chilli. Remember that a little goes a long way.

MIDDLE EASTERN

Pomegranate Molasses: A Persian syrup made from reduced pomegranate juice. It has a sharp sweet and sour flavour, which is an excellent marinade or glaze for lamb, duck, or chicken, or it is delicious used in dressings for couscous, vegetable salads, and grilled aubergines.

INDIAN

Tamarind: A major ingredient in Worcestershire sauce, this sweet and sour ingredient is a key flavour for Indian, Thai, and Mexican cooking. Buy tamarind as blocks of pulp, which are soaked in hot water and then sieved, or use bottled tamarind sold in supermarkets. We adore it in marinades, dipping sauces and dressings.

MEXICAN

Ancho Chillies: Sweet, fruit-flavoured chillies that are mild on the heat scale. They are sold dried and must be reconstituted in boiling water. They lend a beautiful taste to sauces for meats, marinades, and salsas.

Chipotles in Adobo Sauce: These little cans of smoky chillies packed in a garlicky tomato sauce are a must for every kitchen. A powerhouse of hot flavour, the chipotle is actually a dried and smoked jalapeño chilli. Use carefully in dressings, marinades, potato salads, and sauces.

NORTH AFRICAN

Preserved Lemons: These make a lovely addition to tagines, salsas, salads, and marinades, adding a mysterious sweet and sour flavour. Make your own by cutting 5 lemons into quarters, placing in a sealed, sterilised jar with 75g (2¾oz) of sea salt. Cover with lemon juice and leave for 2 weeks. To use, rinse and scoop away the flesh. Finely chop the skin.

Harissa Paste: A powerful wallop of flavour and heat sold in a tiny jar. Made of roasted chilli peppers, coriander, garlic, and olive oil, harissa is fantastic for tagines, couscous, salads, yogurt sauces, salsas, and marinades.

diva**parties**

Preparation is fundamental to making sure you and your guests enjoy your party. If you find yourself worrying about quantities or last minute disasters, you will not have a good time, but with careful forward planning you can relax as much as your guests. For the diva cook, sourcing the best ingredients, the freshest meat, the crispest salads, and the tastiest vegetables, is all part of the fun. Follow our guidelines for menu planning, quantities, shopping, preparation, and storage and you can't fail to have a successful party.

planning

designing your menu

Good menu design ensures the cook never has too much to do and that a variety of guests are catered for.

- Consider your guests' tastes as well as any special dietary requirements.
- Give the party a theme that's easy to design around.
- Plan according to seasonal availability of ingredients.
- Know your budget. If you splurge on a main course, for instance, you may want to economize on others.
- Choose a menu that's convenient to prepare in the time available. Keep in mind the space you have and equipment you'll need.
- Balance colours, textures, and flavours throughout the meal.
- Serving three full courses is no longer de rigueur. Try offering a few canapés as a starter and replacing dessert with fruit and cheese, a good choice for a mid-week party.
- Rely on the party menu suggestions that follow this section – they offer tried and tested themes and a delicious balance of flavours.

knowing your quantities

Preparing too little food can be a disaster, while piles of uneaten dishes can take the shine off what was otherwise a huge success of a party. Following these tips should make sure your guests are well fed and that you've used your party budget wisely.

canapés

- Pre-lunch canapés: 3–4 different canapés, allow 3–4 per head.
- Canapés served as a starter: 4 different canapés, allow 5 per head.
- Evening canapé party: 6–8 different canapés, allow 10 per head.
- Canapés served instead of a meal: 8 different canapés, allow 16 per head.

other dishes

- Guests will consume less food when standing while eating than they do when sitting down, so adjust accordingly.

- When ordering prime cuts of meat or fish, which have no bones or fat, we allow 4 servings to 450g (1lb). This is particularly accurate when using fillet of lamb or beef.
- Don't be tempted to serve too many different dishes, or the unique flavours of each recipe will just merge into one. We feel a spectacular main course dish works well with no more than two side dishes.
- If you are serving canapés or a starter before the main course, don't serve too much – choose a few stunning canapés to take the edge off people's hunger, not fill them up!

shopping

Shopping is all about getting fantastic, really fresh, and exotic ingredients in the right quantities, and with the minimum amount of fuss. Today, buying wonderful food for parties is easier than ever, especially if you follow our guidelines.

- Place your order for meat, fish, and other speciality ingredients 1 week ahead of the event in order to avoid disappointment.
- Try to purchase from local suppliers. The quality is normally high and they often deliver.
- Supermarkets may make home deliveries if you shop via the internet. This is worthwhile when ordering heavy dry goods, drinks, and household products. We don't, however, recommend that you allow a supermarket to choose your meats, vegetables, or other fresh goods. To ensure the best quality, do this in person.
- Organic foods are now widely available and are sometimes, though not always, superior. Be choosy about what you buy to make sure that the product is worth the price. Organic meat and poultry are sure bets for taste, but the quality of vegetables may be inconsistent.
- Think quality, quality and quality again when choosing your meats and produce. But remember: the most expensive doesn't always equate to the best quality. Street markets, farmers' markets, and greengrocers are ideal places for finding superb foods at reasonable prices.
- To avoid repeated, frustrating searches for unusual ethnic ingredients, find a good source, buy large quantities, and store your purchases. If you live far from a metropolitan area, consider ordering these ingredients online and having them sent directly to your home. This can be a godsend!
- Visiting local ethnic grocers is a marvellous adventure. Whether the shop is Greek, Chinese, Thai, Indian, or some other nationality, there's a fascinating new world to discover. You will appreciate the outstanding variety and quality, and you'll learn a thing or two about another culture's cuisine.
- Attempt to shop seasonally, as this affects flavour and prices enormously.
- Buy meat up to 2 days in advance.
- Because fish should be as fresh as possible when eaten, pre-order all fish and seafood and collect on the day you plan to cook.
- Obtain salad, herbs and soft fruits no more than 1 day ahead of your party.
- Purchase winter salad, such as chicory and spinach, 1–2 days before you prepare it.

storage

Once you get your shopping home, it is crucial to store all of the ingredients carefully in order to avoid spoilage.

vegetables and fruit

lettuces Keep in a dark, cool place – a larder or fridge. If refrigerated, place in a large plastic bag and spray with a little water.

root vegetables Store in a dark, cool area for up to 1 week. Remove all plastic wrapping.

onions, shallots and garlic Store in a basket in a dark, cool place for up to 2 weeks. Always remove plastic wrapping or sprouting will begin.

tomatoes Store in a basket at room temperature. Never refrigerate.

herbs Wash and place in a glass of water in the refrigerator. Most will only keep for up to 2 days, with the exception of parsley, which lasts for up to 5 days.

summer fruits Keep cool and dry for 2 days.

hard fruits Store these in a dark, cool area for up to 1 week.

meat, poultry, and fish

meat Chill on a plate, uncovered, for up to 2 days.
fish Chill, loosely covered, for 1-2 days.
poultry Chill, covered for 1-2 days.

dairy

creams Store chilled, loosely covered.
eggs and butter keep in a cool larder.

spices, nuts, oils, and pastes

dry spice Keep in a dry cool place for up to 6 months. Keep dried chillies in a refrigerator in order to prevent brittleness.
oils Store all oils for up to 6 months in a cool dark cupboard. Walnut oil should be refrigerated and used quickly to ensure fragrance.
nuts Store in a dry cool space or refrigerate. Use within 6 months to maintain freshness.
pastes Refrigerate all opened chilli pastes and keep unopened in a dry cool place.

equipment

Though you don't need to purchase every cooking gadget that is available on the market, we hope our recommended list might help as a guide. Many of the items that appear on this list are essential for specific recipes in this book, but others are not essential – they will simply make your life a little easier.

large electric food processor Buy one that does not have so many parts that it's impossible to clean.
sharp citrus fruit squeezer
frying pan A heavy non-stick pan is versatile and long-lasting
knives We recommend your collection includes 1 large heavy chopping knife, 1 small serrated knife and 1 long carving knife. Purchase the best quality that you can afford and be sure to sharpen your knife blades regularly.
vegetable peeler There are many styles; use what feels most comfortable to you.
sharp cheese and citrus fruit grater and zester Try to find a grater that grates finely, but is a normal shape.
food scales with ounces and grams
large chopping boards Keep separate boards for meat and vegetables.
cake tins Removable-base springform tins, 20cm (8–9in) wide.
tart tins Choose fluted, loose-bottomed 20cm (8in) tins.
a cake mixer This may be a bit extravagant, but it lasts a lifetime and is particularly good for whisking egg whites very stiff.
roasting tins Large, high-quality tins will last longer.
individual 10cm (4in) cake tins These are useful for making tarte tatins, both savoury and sweet.

electric hand whisk Use it to whisk both egg whites and
whipping cream.

electric deep-fat fryer Choose a well-known brand that
is easy to refill and clean.

large fine sieve Transferring ingredients into a tiny sieve
can be a nightmare, so choose a good-sized one.

a large colander Small sizes are not as useful, for the
reason as for sieves. Large colanders are ideal for drip-
drying washed salad leaves and efficiently draining
vegetables and pasta.

a salad spinner There is no better way to thoroughly dry
salad leaves so as not to dilute the dressing. Otherwise
use a large clean and dry tea-towel to carefully shake the
lettuce leaves dry.

mini muffin tins A non-stick 12 muffin capacity tin is
essential for making wonton cups and filo tartlets.

pastry brush Since they often lose bristles, either purchase
a brush of superior quality or be prepared to buy many of
cheaper construction.

biscuit cutters Plain-edged cutters are probably the most
useful. It makes good sense to buy a little tin that includes
a variety of sizes.

preparation and cooking schedule

Endless lists of ingredients to be
bought and dishes to be prepared may
seem daunting, but with simple planning
even apparently complex menus can be
disarmingly straightforward.

1 week ahead

• Choose your menu and write out your shopping lists.

• Pre-order any important ingredients, such as meat, fish,
fresh herbs.

• Write out a cooking preparation timetable for
your party.

• If you are serving recipes that include pastry, you
can make the pastry, line the pastry case, and freeze
it uncooked.

• You can make crostini, filo tartlets, and other cases,
and store in an airtight, dry container.

• Breads can be made, frozen, and then reheated when
you are ready to serve them.

2 days ahead

• Do your party shopping.

• Make any vinaigrettes or dressings and keep covered in
a cool place.

• Slow braised meat dishes or soups are far better
made several days in advance. Cover and store in
the fridge.

• Both pestos and tapenades can be prepared
ahead and then kept in an airtight container in a
cool place.

• Vegetable mashes and purees can be prepared, chilled
and reheated to serve.

• Our potato cake recipes work brilliantly made ahead and
chilled. Fry to serve.

• Rice and couscous dishes can also be prepared ahead
as long as you ensure that you cover well, chill, and reheat
thoroughly when serving.

1 day ahead

- Fresh herbs and salads can be washed, dried well, and chilled in large, airy plastic bags.
- Pick up any last-minute ingredients such as cheeses, breads, fruits, and fish.
- Marinate your meat, cover and chill, making sure that you turn the meat over in the marinade several times during the marinating time.
- Prepare vegetables and chill – be sure to keep root vegetables in cold water.
- Salsas and sauces that are appropriate can be made – leave out the fresh herbs until ready to serve.
- Make your dessert, as most can be made successfully a day ahead.
- Finish off baking any tarts that can be served cold or reheated.
- Vegetables can be blanched in salted water, drained and submerged into iced water. Dry on kitchen paper, wrap, and refrigerate.

a few hours ahead

- Assemble cold canapés and leave garnishing until last.
- Decorate any cold desserts and leave in a cool place, but do not add such things as mint leaves until last as they will absorb the mint flavour almost immediately.
- Fish can be seared several hours ahead. Simply brown it, chill immediately, and roast it just before serving.
- Sear the meat several hours ahead, ready to roast.
- Complete roasting the meat about 15 minutes before the meal, then allow it to rest for 10–15 minutes. Carve only to serve.
- Roast or blanch vegetables. Keep them warm or reheat to serve.
- Deep-fry any fried foods, drain on kitchen paper and keep warm in a medium to low oven to serve.
- Garnish foods with herbs just as you serve them to avoid them wilting.
- Assemble salads as late as possible to keep them fresh and light in appearance.

menu ideas

Planning exactly what dishes you want to match to create a party menu can be time-consuming and exhausting with so many fabulous diva dishes to choose from! So here's a list of a few of our favourites – we're sure they'll work as wonderfully for you as they have for us!

prepare ahead party menu

Golden shallot pancakes with garlic and green olive tapenade
Goats cheese baked in spicy tomato sauce with garlic crostini
Gingered beef with honey and prunes
Pineapple and star anise tarte tatin

last minute party food for fast lives

Tomato bruschetta with asparagus, gorgonzola and basil salad
Seared tuna steaks with couscous and Sicilian vinaigrette
Chez panise chocolate cake

a taste of the orient

Vietnamese porkballs with lettuce wraps
Thai green papaya salad with seared chilli prawns
Skewered Thai chicken with tomato chilli jam
Fresh fig and plum tarte tatin

mexican fiesta

Spiced corncakes with avocado-lime salsa
Tuna seviche with mango and red onion salsa with tortilla chips
Smoky chipotle chicken with grilled pineapple salsa
Black bean tacos with cherry tomato salsa
Cinnamon pavlovas with carmelised apples

summer sizzlers

Sunblushed tomato-chilli pesto with crispy pitta breadsticks
Avocado and goat's cheese crostini with roasted cherry tomatoes

Chargrilled Mediterranean chicken with roasted garlic
and basil dressing
Heavenly chunky chewy chocolate cookies

winter warmer
Smoked trout on toasted walnut bread with parsley and
caper salsa
Caramelized red onion and fennel tarte tatin with olives
and thyme
Monkfish, bacon and dill pie with parmesan and spring
onion mash
Cinnamon pavlova with caramelized apples

an extravagant affair
Smoked salmon in filo cups with roasted pepper, dill, and
lime salsa
Fennel and seafood bouillabaisse with saffron aioli
Seared duck breasts with balsamic, rosemary, and
shallot sauce
Sweet potato and ginger mash
Lavender-honey mascarpone crème brûlée

a perfectly portable picnic
Sunblushed tomato-chilli pesto with crisy pitta breadsticks
Spicy grilled prawn skewers with Moroccan tomato jam
Parsley and roasted garlic tart
Greek chicken salad with caper and anchovy vinaigrette
Fennel slaw with dill and cider dressing
Miniature foccacia topped with caramelized onions
Heavenly chunky chewy chocolate cookies

a party menu that freezes
Smoked fish tart with crème fraiche, lemon, and parmesan
Balsamic chicken with porcini mushrooms
Chez panise chocolate cake

alfesco B.B.Q menu
Grilled prawns with tamarind recado and avocado-red
onion relish
Seared fillet of lamb with spiced, roasted garlic, and
yogurt sauce
Tuscan panzanella salad
Bababganoush salad with goat's cheese and crispy pitta
New York cheesecake with fresh summer berries

formal dinner for 8
Asian gravadlax with chilli crème fraîche.
Marinated fig, glazed shallot, and prosciutto with
parmesan crisps
Fillet of beef with coriander-peanut pesto
Baby green salad with beetroot, spring onion, and sesame
Caramelized new potatoes with tomato and soy
Chocolate, amaretti, and brandy meringue roulade

canapés for a crowd
Filo tartlets of seared duck with sweet tomato-sesame
chutney
Mini caesar salad on croute
Spiced corncakes with avocado-lime salsa
Sri Lankan fishcakes with tomato sambal
Warm gorgonzola wontons
Gingered chicken cakes with coriander sauce

keep it hot – spicy party food
Crispy crab and cheese wontons with sweet chilli
dipping sauce
Asian gravadlax with chilli crème fraîche
Prawn, lime, and ginger spring rolls with peanut dipping sauce
Thai beef salad
Asian potato cakes with chilli sambal
Korean chicken with cucumber salad
Sweet goat's cheese, orange and almond tart

think thai
Prawn dumplings in fragrant Thai broth with Thai basil
Spicy crabcakes with tomato-coriander salsa
Skewered Thai chicken with chilli jam
Carmelised new potatoes with tomato and soy sauce
Pineapple and star anise tarte tatin

terrific pacific
Cucumber cups with Thai prawns
Grilled Indonesian coconut curried chicken
Tamarind roasted vegetables
Fresh fig and plum tarte tatin

tuscan nights
Tuscan panzanella salad
Spiedini of scallops with chunky salsa verde

Slow roasted Tuscan pork with fennel and chilli salt rub.

Celeriac and roasted garlic puree

Glazed fruits with almond biscotti and crème fraîche.

elegent evening

Filo tarts of smoked salmon, tomato, and dill with cucumber-lime salsa

Gingered chicken cakes with coriander sauce

Braised duck legs with soy, ginger, and star anise

Carmelized new potatoes with tomato and soy sauce

Lavender-honey mascarpone crème brûlée

in praise of the tomato, a late summer's menu

Roasted tomato-shallot tarte tatin

Butterflied leg of lamb with slow roasted tomato, basil and olive confit

Saffron roasted potatoes with rosemary and red onions

Pistachio nut and berry meringue roulade

a japanese influenced menu

Cucumber cups with Thai prawns

Grilled teriyaki fillet of beef with green tea noodles and ginger-mustard dipping sauce

Miso glazed cod

Chez Panisse chocolate cake

indelibly indian

Vegetable pakoras with coriander chutney

Filo tartlets of seared duck with sweet tomato and sesame chutney

Seared scallops and monkfish on spiced red lentils with yogurt sauce

Cinnamon pavlovas with summer berries

very vegetarian menu

Polenta crusted aubergine, roasted tomatoes, buffalo mozzarella, and salsa verde dressing

Wild mushroom and smoked mozzarella tart

Baby leaf salad with beetroot, spring onion and sesame

Chocolate amaretti roulade

middle eastern magic

Babganoush salad with goat's cheese

Mezze salad plate

Spiced cumin flatbread

Lemon coriander tabouli with marinated pomegranate lamb cutlets

Pistachio nut-berry meringue roulade

gaucho grill

Spiced chicken empanadas with green chilli sauce

Mojo marinated steak with coriander sauce and green

Chilean salsa

Sweet goat's cheese and almond tart

moroccan mystique

Spicy grilled prawn skewers with Moroccan

tomato jam

Filo tart with chermoula chicken

Moroccan carrots

Cinnamon pavlovas with caramelized apples

veggies do lunch

Marinated fig, glazed shallot, and proscuitto salad

with parmesan crisps (proscuitto would be omitted)

Roasted tomato tarte tatin

Winter squash and blue cheese galette

Diva breadsticks

Heavenly chunky chewy chocolate cookies

pure mediterranean extravaganza

Golden shallot pancakes with green olive tapenade

Spinach salad with crispy pancetta and warm

garlic dressing

Grilled red pepper stuffed with herbed ricotta and black

olive vinaigrette

Spiedini of scallops with a chunky salsa verde

Double chocolate mascarpone tart

indian vegetarian feast

Vegetable pakoras with coriander chutney and tamarind

dipping sauce

Roasted winter vegetables in a fragrant coconut sauce

Coconut rice

Cumin flatbread

Pistachio-berry meringue roulade

quick and elegant

Warm roquefort wontons

Grilled swordfish with rosemary, tomato, and

carmelized onions

Baby green salad with classic vinaigrette

Chez Panisse chocolate cake

veggies go to the middle east

Mezze salad plate

Babaganoush salad with goat's cheese and crispy pita bread

Moroccan carrots

Couscous with roasted sweet potatoes and harissa dressing

Sweet goat's cheese, orange, and almond tart

elegant autumn dinner

Mini Caesar salad en croute

Gratin of balsamic wild mushrooms

Butterflied leg of lamb with slow roasted tomato confit

Saffron roasted potatoes with rosemary and red onions

Winter glazed fruits with biscotti and crème fraîche

cool and refreshing for summer

Cucumber cups with Thai prawns

Vietnamese minced chicken salad with citrus mint dressing

Grilled prawns with Tamarind and avocado/red onion salsa

Soba noodle salad with shredded aubergine and soy

balsamic dressing

New York cheesecake with fresh blueberries

brunch for a bunch

Chargrilled Mediterranean chicken with roasted garlic

and basil dressing

Tuscan panzanella salad

Broccoli rabe, Italian sausage, and pecorino tart with

roasted cherry tomatoes

Filo tartlets of smoked salmon, tomato, and dill/

cucumber salsa

Pistachio berry meringue roulade

index

aioli 73, 85

apples: caramelized 145; glazed 147

asparagus, gorgonzola and basil salad 98

aubergines: with goat's cheese and tomato galette 43; polenta-crusted 100; pureed 122; roasted with soba noodle salad 119

avocado-goat's cheese crostini 8

avocado-lime salsa 17

babaganoush salad with goat's cheese 108

baking ingredients 148-9

balsamic vinegar 74, 75, 109

basil 64, 112, 117, 172

beans, black bean tacos 103

beef 62; chilli-crusted beef fillet 60; gingered, with honey and prunes 65; mojo-marinated steaks with coriander sauce and Chilean salsa 61; roast fillet with coriander and peanut pesto 66; teriyaki 54; Thai beef salad 126

biscuits see cookies

breads: breadsticks 11, 158; bruschetta 98; ciabatta 123; crostini 8, 21, 111; croûte 15; cumin flatbread 163; focaccia 161; olive oil and sea salt 158, 160; pitta 11, 108; sourdough 98, 123; star toast 23; toasted walnut 18

broccoli, sausage and Pecorino tart 53

canapés 8-37

carrots, Moroccan 133

celeriac, and roasted garlic puree 131

cheesecake, New York cheesecake 143

cheeses: blue 117; cheddar in potato cakes 104; cream cheese 24, 106, 149; dolcelatte 98; goat's cheese 8, 43, 108, 111, 140, 149; gorgonzola 50, 98; Gruyère 109; mascarpone 142, 149, 150; mozzarella 10, 41, 53, 100; Parmesan 11, 21, 44, 45, 47, 93, 109, 117, 125, 158; Pecorino 53; Provolone 109; ricotta 14, 106; Roquefort 14

chicken 76-7; balsamic chicken with porcini mushrooms and sun-dried cherries 75; brochettes of lemon chicken 73; char-grilled Mediterranean chicken 112; charmoula chicken 52; empanaditas 30; gingered chicken cakes 34; Greek chicken salad 114; grilled Indonesian coconut chicken 78; Korean barbecue chicken 71; seared Thai chicken 80; smoky chipotle chicken 79; Vietnamese minced chicken salad 115

chillies 20, 117, 173; ancho 60, 175; chilli crème fraîche 23; chilli prawns 120; chipotle 79, 82, 175; fillings for breadsticks 158; harissa 11, 105, 175; sweet chilli bean paste 174; sweet chilli dipping sauce 175; Thai chilli sauce 24; tomato-chilli jam 80

chocolate 149; and amaretti meringue roulade 154; Chez Panisse chocolate cake 155; cookies 156

chutneys see pickles, chutneys and relishes

cinnamon 173; pavlovas 145

coconut: with grilled chicken 78; rice 139; sauce 101

cod 91; miso glazed 92

confits: garlic and rosemary 158; tomato, basil and olive 64

cookies, chocolate 156

coriander 117, 172; and cherry tomato salsa 84; and mint dipping sauce 12; and peanut pesto 66; with roasted garlic and yogurt sauce 56; sauce 34, 61; seeds 117, 173; tabbouleh 59

corn cakes, spiced, with avocado-lime salsa 17

couscous: with roasted sweet potato 105; with seared tuna 95

crab 90; and cream cheese wontons 24; spicy crab cakes 84

crème brulée 142

crème fraîche 23, 45, 70, 117, 148

cucumber: cucumber relish 89; cucumber salad 71; cucumber-lime salsa 49; cups and ribbons 21, 29

desserts 140-56

dressings see sauces and dressings

duck 76; braised duck legs with soy, ginger & star anise 68; seared breasts with balsamic vinegar, rosemary & shallot sauce 74; seared with tomato-sesame chutney in filo tartlets 37

equipment 167-8

fennel 85; seed 117, 158, 173; slaw 134

figs: marinated, with glazed shallot and prosciutto salad 125; and plum tarte tatin 152

fish & seafood 82-97; canapés 18-19, 22-9, 32; smoked fish 18, 19, 45, 49, 91; Sri Lankan fish cakes 22; tarts 45, 49

flavours 47, 116, 117; ethnic 174-5

fruit 21, 75, 145, 146, 149; winter glazed 147

fudge sauce 152

garlic: roasted 38, 50, 56, 112, 131; and rosemary confit 158

garnishes 20-1

ginger 20, 21, 173; ginger mustard dipping sauce 54; gingered beef with honey and prunes 65; gingered chicken cakes 34; and sweet potato mash 130; with sweet potato & prawn fritters 89

gravadlax, Asian on star toast 23

Guinea fowl 77; breasts with tarragon and crème fraîche 70

herbs 20, 117, 172-3

honey 65, 116; and mascarpone crème brulée 142

lamb 62-3; butterflied leg with slow-roasted tomato, basil & olive confit 64; fillet with roasted garlic, coriander & yogurt sauce 56; pomegranate-marinated cutlets & coriander tabbouleh 59

marinades: for meat 54, 59, 61, 62-3, 64, 66; for fish/seafood 82, 92, 97, 120; for poultry 52, 71, 74, 76-7, 78, 80, 114

meat dishes 54-66; canapés 35

meringue 145, 146, 154

mint 12, 26, 172

monkfish 85, 91, 93, 96

mushrooms: ancho and mushroom sauce 60; dried 174; gratin of balsamic wild mushrooms 109; porcini 75; wild mushroom and smoked mozzarella tart 41

noodles, soba 119

nuts 146, 149

oils 116, 175

olives 10, 64, 106, 117, 158, 174

onions 40, 97, 158, 161

pakoras, with dipping sauces 12

pancakes, shallot with garlic and green olive tapenade 10

parties, planning, preparation and menus 164-71

pastry 46-8, see also under canapés, tarts and tarte tatin

pavlovas, cinnamon 145

peanuts 26, 66

pears, glazed 147

peppers: grilled pepper salad 122; grilled red peppers stuffed with herb ricotta 106; red pepper aioli 73; roasted pepper & dill salsa 19

pesto 11, 66

pickles, chutneys and relishes: cucumber relish 89; Moroccan tomato jam 27, 52; pickled ginger 20; red onion and pomegranate relish 65; tomato-chilli jam 80; tomato-sesame chutney 37

pineapple: salsas 79, 82; tarte tatin with star anise 151

plums: and fresh fig tarte tatin 152; glazed 147

polenta-crusted aubergines 100

pomegranate 59, 65

pomegranate molasses 116, 175

pork 63; slow-roasted Tuscan with fennel 57; Vietnamese grilled in lettuce parcels 35

potatoes: Asian potato cakes 104; caramelized new potatoes 136; mashed with spring onion and Parmesan 93; saffron-roasted 138, see also sweet potato

poultry dishes 68-80; canapés 24, 30, 37

prawns 85, 90; grilled with tamarind and pineapple & red onion salsa 82; with Moroccan tomato jam 27; prawn dumplings in fragrant Thai broth 88; prawn, mint and ginger spring rolls 26; seared chilli prawns with a papaya salad 120; with sweet potato & ginger fritters 89; Thai prawns in cucumber cups 29

prosciutto 73, 125, 158

puddings 140-56

relishes see pickles, chutneys and relishes

rice, fluffy coconut rice 139

rice vinegar 135

rosemary 20, 74, 97, 158, 172

roulades 146, 154

saffron 85, 138, 173

salads 112-27; asparagus, gorgonzola & basil 98; babaganoush 108; baby green salad with beetroot, spring onion & sesame 135; Caesar salad 15; char-grilled Mediterranean chicken 112; chickpea 122; Chinese chicken 31; cucumber 71; Greek chicken 114; grilled pepper 122; marinated figs with glazed shallot & prosciutto 125; mezze plate 122; panzanella salad 123; soba noodle salad with roasted aubergine 119; Thai beef 126; Thai green papaya 120; Vietnamese minced chicken 115

salmon: gravadlax 23; smoked 19, 49

salsa: avocado-lime 17; cherry tomato 84, 103; Chilean 61; cucumber-lime 49; mango 32; parsley-caper 18; pineapple 79; pineapple and red onion 82; roasted pepper and dill 19; salsa verde 87, 100, see also sauces and dressings; vinaigrettes

sambals 22, 104, 175

sauces and dressings 116-18; adobo 79, 82, 175; ancho and mushroom 60; balsamic, rosemary & shallot 74; balsamic wild mushroom 109; caper & anchovy vinaigrette 114; cider vinegar 134; coconut 101; coriander 34; dipping 12, 24, 26, 54, 175; fudge 152; green chilli 30; harissa 105; mayonnaise 118; rice vinegar & soy sauce 135; roasted garlic & basil 15; rosemary, tomato and caramelized onions 97; saffron 138; for salads 115, 123; soy-balsamic 119; spicy tomato 111; Thai chilli 24; yogurt 56, 96, 105, 117, see also salsa; vinaigrettes

sausage, Italian 53

scallops 85, 87, 90, 96

seafood see fish and seafood dishes

shellfish see fish and seafood dishes

soba noodle salad with roasted aubergine 119

soups: bouillabaisse 85; Thai broth with prawn dumplings 88

spices 117, 173

spring rolls, Thai 26

squash, butternut, with roasted garlic, and gorgonzola galette 50

sweet potatoes 89, 101, 105, 128, 130, see also potatoes

swordfish 91, 97

tabbouleh 59

tacos, smoky black bean tacos 103

tamarind 175; dipping sauce 12; glaze 128

tapenade, green olive 10

tarte tatin: fresh fig and plum 152; onion and fennel 40; pineapple 151; roasted tomato and shallot 44

tarts 38-53; aubergine, goat's cheese and tomato galette 43; broccoli, sausage and Pecorino 53; charmoula chicken 52; double chocolate mascarpone 150; parsley and roasted garlic tart 38; seared duck 37; smoked fish 45; smoked salmon 19, 49; sweet goat's cheese, orange and almond 140; wild mushroom and smoked mozzarella tart 41; winter squash, with roasted garlic, and gorgonzola galette 50

teriyaki beef fillet with noodles 54

tomatoes 8, 11, 20, 43, 53, 117; galette 43; jams chutneys & confits 27, 37, 52, 64, 80; with polenta-crusted aubergines 100; roasted tomato & shallot tarte tatin 44; sauces, salsas & sambals 22, 84, 97, 103, 104, 111; tomato bruschetta 98

tortillas 32

trout, smoked 18

tuna 91; seared 95; tuna ceviche on corn tortillas 32

vegetables: extra side dishes 128-39; roasted winter vegetables in coconut sauce 101

vegetarian dishes 98-111

vinaigrettes 95, 106, 114, 116-18, 125, 126, 133, see also salsa; sauces

vinegars 116, 134, 135

wontons 14, 24, 31

yogurt 56, 96, 105, 117, 149